SUZANNE GIBBS

THE
Pressure Cooker
RECIPE BOOK

VIKING

an imprint of

PENGUIN BOOKS

Contents

Introduction   1

Nibbles & light meals   11

Stocks & soups   35

Vegetables   57

Grains & pulses   79

One-pot dinners   101

Braises & casseroles   121

Desserts   153

Acknowledgements   182

Index   183

Introduction

It's not the snowy slopes that I remember most from a skiing holiday spent at Kosciusko with my mother in the mid-1950s. Nor is it the evening meals enjoyed with family friends in the chalet that will stand out in my memories of that trip. It is the enormously loud explosion that occurred one night as our dinner shot through the air, sending us all racing out into the cold: somehow, someone had lifted the lid off my mother's pressure cooker. From that moment, pressure cookers were off my must-have list of kitchen appliances.

Throughout my life, exchanging ideas about food has forged many stimulating new friendships. I began such a friendship four years ago, when fellow Le Cordon Bleu graduate Lucy Nunes came to work with me. Lucy grew up in Paris and, although she says I have taught her much, I will be forever grateful for what she has taught me.

'Suzanne,' she said one day, 'don't you have a pressure cooker?'

'Heavens no!' I said. 'They're so dangerous.'

'You know, most French households have a pressure cooker,' she said, and with this, she sparked an idea. The conversation encouraged me to give pressure cookers another go; if they were good enough for the French, well, they couldn't be so bad.

So I bought my first pressure cooker: a 6-litre, stainless-steel beauty. It's quite nice-looking, and holds pride of place on my stovetop, where it is used nearly every day. There's been three years' of trial since then, and although there's been a fair amount of 'error', there have been many more successes to report.

The pressure cooker has brought back into my life those delicious braises and stews that used to bubble away on the stove for hours. Now I think nothing of making a melt-in-the-mouth osso bucco or a French daube at the drop of a hat. Those many hours of long, slow cooking have miraculously turned into half an hour. A great bolognese sauce that used to take three hours now takes just twenty-five minutes.

There are other great benefits too. The pressure cooker is the perfect vehicle for cooking cheaper, but usually more flavoursome cuts of meat, like chuck, shoulder and braising steak, as well as dried beans, peas and lentils. Pressure-cooked food is succulent and full of flavour, and pressure cooking tenderises the toughest meats.

Pressure-cooked food is also healthy. Today's pressure cookers have advanced pressure-regulating systems, eliminating the need for a lot of water, and because the food requires less cooking liquid, more vitamins and minerals are retained and vegetables have more flavour and colour. There are also environmental benefits to using a pressure cooker. Since modern pressure cookers save around 70 per cent of the cooking time, less energy is needed and less heat is generated – an added bonus in hot weather.

My stainless-steel pressure cooker is very different from my mother's old aluminium time-bomb. With its spring valve, there's not a chance you can open it until the pressure is released. Pressure cookers are now as safe as houses (even in ski chalets!), easy to use, and once you've become familiar with the types of foods that are best cooked in them, you'll find there's no end to the variety of dishes you can create. I've come a long way in my thinking since my childhood experience in the Kosciusko chalet.

We're all working harder. We like to eat well, but most of us are unable to spend all our days joyfully in the kitchen. Once you've got the hang of it, the pressure cooker will be your favourite kitchen companion, and the perfect tool for fast, delicious, nutritious and economical home-cooked meals.

Pressure cooking: how does it work?

Most of us can drive a car without a detailed understanding of what makes it go, and so it is with using pressure cookers. You could cook this way without really understanding much about how they work, so long as you follow the manufacturer's guidelines. But a bit of knowledge about this cooking technique can make the process much more satisfying – and you won't need a physics degree, either!

Pressure cooking is a way of cooking food in liquid using a gasket-sealed pan to retain steam and build pressure. By increasing the pressure inside the pan, the boiling point of the liquid in the pressure cooker is raised to 120–125°C, some 20–25°C higher than normal boiling point. The increased temperature of the water and steam causes the fibres of the food to break down more quickly, and shortens the cooking time by up to 70 per cent.

Most modern pressure cookers are designed for use on a gas or electric stovetop, and pressure cookers made from stainless steel can also be used on induction and ceramic stovetops. During cooking, you adjust the burner on your stove to maintain the required pressure as registered by the valve, or regulator, on the lid of the pressure cooker. If the pressure cooker is overheated, or the valve becomes blocked, excess steam will be automatically released through a vent, or through a safety valve if both the valve and vent

Second-generation pressure cookers come in all shapes and sizes.

become blocked. When the pressure cooker is removed from the heat and starts to cool, the steam condenses, the pressure inside the pan is lost and the lid can then be safely opened.

Choosing the right pressure cooker for you

Today's second-generation pressure cookers are very efficient and include many features and safety mechanisms that didn't exist on earlier models. All the stainless-steel pressure cookers available today are of comparable quality and have similar safety systems. What sets them apart from each other is their varying features and size. Generally, you get what you pay for in terms of speed, ease of use and pressure control. Just make sure the model you choose includes a manual with clear, detailed operating instructions and a good selection of basic recipes.

Aluminium or stainless steel?

Although aluminium cookers are considerably cheaper, I would recommend opting for stainless steel, as it is easier to clean and more durable. All modern stainless-steel pressure cookers have heatproof handles and a thick aluminium 3-ply 'sandwich' base, which evenly distributes heat and prevents hot spots forming.

Large or small?

In choosing a pressure cooker you need to consider the size of your family, how often you cook, and what you like to cook. With a bigger pressure cooker (7–9 litres) you can cook a large quantity of food so you'll have enough left over for another meal. This size is very versatile as it can accommodate a good-sized chicken, a pot roast or a cheesecake, and can also double as a stockpot. Down the track you may want to have two pressure cookers, one large and one small, so you can cook rice and meat or vegies at the same time. One shape I like in the new range of pressure cookers is the 25 cm pressure frying pan. Its shallower sides make it perfect for browning meat in, which can be tricky in a larger, deeper cooker. It's great for braising small joints or a couple of pork chops, or for making a quick Spanish-style chicken with rice. If you are thinking of buying a second pressure cooker, or if you just want one small cooker (and don't intend to cook soups in it), this would be a good choice.

One handle or two?

To my mind, the best cookers have handles on both sides of the pot, rather than a single, long handle. They're much easier and safer to carry to the sink when you need to cool the cooker down quickly. (Some have smaller 'assist' or 'helper' handles for this purpose.) Before you buy, practise locking and opening the lid on several models – you'll probably find some are easier than others.

Which brand?

You can buy pressure cookers at most department stores and selected kitchenware retailers. To get you started, here are some of the leading brands:

Kuhn Rikon (kuhnrikon.com) – This Swiss company invented the spring-loaded valve system that makes today's pressure cookers perfectly safe and quiet. These cookers are top of the range and have all the added features, including multiple back-up safety systems.

Tefal 'Clipso' (tefal.com.au) – Made in France under the French brand SEB, their main feature is a simple one-touch opening and locking operation of the lid. They also have a dial-up pressure selection and an automatic timing mechanism.

Evinox 'Rapid' and 'Europe' – Made in Portugal, these cookers offer maximum safety, versatility and excellent value. The 'Europe' model incorporates flame guards for long life on gas burners, and has a smaller handle for easier storage.

Fagor (fagoramerica.com) – Made in Spain, these have all the features of modern pressure cookers and a contemporary European-style design.

Fissler 'Blue Point' and 'Vitavit Royal' (fissler.net) – These excellent cookers are made in Germany and have four independent safety pressure-release systems.

WMF 'Perfect' (wmf.com) – A top-quality range of pressure cookers made in Germany. A key feature of this range is that the lid handle, containing the pressure mechanism, is removable, so you can clean the lid as well as the pan in the dishwasher.

Using your pressure cooker

Please note: Before you begin to use your pressure cooker, it's very important that you read the instruction manual and fully understand the safety features of your particular cooker.

The basic principle of this type of cooking involves heating ingredients in some form of liquid in a sealed pan. The liquid (be it water, stock, wine or verjuice) is essential to create the steam to bring the pot to pressure. The amount of liquid required will depend on the length of cooking time and the ingredients used. For braises, casseroles, soups and the like, the prepared ingredients and liquid are put straight into the cooker (some braises and casseroles require the meat to be browned first for optimum flavour). To steam vegetables on their own (not as part of a soup

Some of the equipment you'll need when using your pressure cooker. It's important that you read and understand the safety instructions for your particular cooker before you begin to use it.

or casserole), place them on a trivet or in a steamer basket and add water to the bottom of the pressure cooker to create steam. Puddings and cakes are cooked in a pudding basin or dish that sits on the trivet. This prevents the cooking vessel from coming into contact with the base of the cooker and burning. The vessel is covered with foil or simply a heatproof plate which seals it and ensures the steam is contained. Again, the steam is created by pouring water straight into the bottom of the cooker.

Once all the ingredients are added, the lid should be tightly sealed. Go gently when turning the lid to the locking position; if you are too heavy-handed or do not align it properly, you could damage the gasket (but don't worry, gaskets are easily replaceable and very simple to remove and put back on).

Most pressure cookers have two pressure levels: high pressure, which is suitable for cooking a wide range of foods; and low pressure, which is more suited

A trivet is used for steaming vegetables, cakes and puddings.

Seal your dish or pudding basin with foil or a heatproof plate.

to delicate foods like chicken breasts, fish and spinach. Once the lid is locked, turn the heat to high to achieve your desired pressure level as soon as possible. Once pressure has been reached (indicated by the valve on the lid of your cooker), you'll need to reduce the heat to keep the pressure stabilised. You may need to use a simmer mat or a smaller burner to reduce the heat enough to maintain pressure. For electric stoves, it's helpful to set one burner on high and a second one on a lower heat: you can bring the cooker up to pressure on the high-heat burner and then move it to the second burner for the remaining cooking time.

Start timing the cooking from the moment the required pressure is reached – use a timer to ensure accuracy. Depending on the amount of food or liquid used, it can take anywhere from 30 seconds to 15 minutes for the cooker to reach full pressure. If you want to speed things up, heat any liquids before adding

The cold-water release method stops the cooking process almost immediately.

them to the cooker. Once pressure is reached, there should be just a soft, gentle hissing sound, or almost no sound at all, coming from the cooker.

There are three ways to release the pressure at the end of the cooking time. The natural-release method, where the cooker is taken off the heat source and left to cool gradually until the pressure releases on its own, is preferable for most dishes as it is gentler on the food and more energy efficient, reducing vapour, odour and water usage. This method is especially suitable for beef, which toughens when pressure is released too quickly, and for those foods with skins you want to keep intact, like beans or potatoes.

If you do need to reduce the pressure quickly to add more ingredients or to check food for done-ness, use the quick-release method by simply turning the dial on your cooker. Another way to quickly release pressure is to carefully transfer the pressure cooker to the sink

and run cold water over the lid, away from the vents or regulator (the cold-water release method). This method is good for foods that need a short cooking time, like fish or delicate vegetables, or foods that should not be overcooked, such as rice or eggs, as it stops the cooking process almost immediately.

Only once the pressure has been released will you be able to open the lid of your pressure cooker. When removing the lid, turn it to unlock, then flip the lid to a vertical position facing away from you to protect yourself from the escaping steam.

Clean your pressure cooker thoroughly after each use. Remove the gasket from the lid and simply wash the lid and base with hot, soapy water (do not soak). Most stainless-steel pressure cooker bases can go in the dishwasher (but check the instruction manual of your particular cooker beforehand to make sure). Never put a pressure cooker lid in the dishwasher as this will damage the valve.

Always lift the lid facing away from you to protect yourself from the steam.

Make sure your pressure cooker is completely dry, inside and out, before putting it away. Store with the lid on upside down to allow the air to circulate and prevent any food odours accumulating.

Safety first

The pressure cookers of today are a far cry from their predecessors, those thin-based aluminium models with hissing jiggler valves that often clogged, resulting in the occasional lid flying off. These days, locking lids prevent pressure building if they aren't properly sealed, and multiple safety valves release steam if the pressure gets too high. The legendary kitchen mishaps such as the one I experienced on my skiing holiday are, thankfully, a thing of the past. In my four years of using a modern pressure cooker, I've never felt I had a time-bomb ticking away on the stove, and I'm happy to report that I've never had a lid fly off or an explosion of potatoes all over the ceiling!

However, as with all cooking, a little common sense is needed. These few basic guidelines will ensure you avoid any mishaps:

- Always remember that you can't fill the cooker to capacity; usually the maximum fill line is one-half to two-thirds of the way up the side, and this should be clearly marked on the inside of the cooker.

- Keep your mind on the job. Don't leave the house or make that telephone call you've put off when there's a pressure cooker on the stove – it should not be left unattended for too long as the heat level needs to be carefully regulated. While it won't blow up, if the heat gets too high, steam will be released through the safety valves and all the liquid inside the cooker could evaporate, possibly damaging it.

- Lifting steamer inserts, bowls or dishes from a hot pressure cooker can be dangerous. I always place a folded tea towel under the cooking vessel so that I can carefully lift things in and out of the cooker. To do this, place the covered pudding basin or dish on a folded tea towel or piece of muslin. Pick up the ends of the cloth, lift the cooking vessel and carefully lower it onto the trivet in the cooker. Fold the ends of the cloth over the vessel and close and lock the lid. At the end of the cooking time, release the pressure and open the lid. Use tongs to pull out the ends of the cloth over the sides of the cooker to cool. After a few seconds, pick up the cloth ends and carefully use them to lift the vessel from the cooker.

- Foods that tend to froth and foam should not be cooked in a pressure cooker. These include pasta, porridge, apple sauce or cranberries. Rhubarb is not suitable when cooked on its own, but can be cooked in a pudding (see page 179).

Use a folded tea towel to safely lift cakes and puddings from the cooker.

What cooks best in the pressure cooker?

Because I'm such a big fan of pressure cooking I'd like to be able to tell you that everything can be cooked this way. But because I'm also a very careful and caring cook, I'm well aware of its strengths and limitations. Pressure cookers are brilliant for foods that need long, slow cooking and moist heat. Quick-cooking foods like fish and very delicate vegetables are generally better prepared by other methods. And when it comes to desserts, anything that contains a substantial amount of flour can become heavy. There are a few puddings, however, that work very well, so I've included recipes for a selection of these.

In short, the following foods are best suited to the pressure cooker.

Soups, stocks, stews, casseroles and long-cooking sauces like ragu alla Bolognese will develop a fabulous rich flavour in 20 minutes or even less. This is because the pressure cooker is so efficient at extracting flavour from meat and bones.

Tough cuts of meats with plenty of flavour such as chuck, gravy or shin of beef, beef cheeks, veal shanks, oxtail, corned beef, lamb shanks and pork shoulder. You can cook a tender, melt-in-the-mouth osso bucco with meat that is falling off the bone in just 25 minutes.

Dried beans become tender, plump and fabulous-tasting when cooked in the pressure cooker. Once you're familiar with the simple technique, you won't bother with canned beans again. For best results, beans should be soaked for a few hours or overnight if possible.

Rice and other grains work really well – brown rice takes just 20 minutes to cook compared to 45 minutes when cooked the conventional way. Risotto is a dream cooked in the pressure cooker. Though there will be some that say pressure-cooked risotto doesn't have the same complexity of flavour, I disagree, and I love the fact that I can put together a delicious dish that is usually so time-consuming at the drop of a hat.

Sturdy, firm vegetables such as beetroot, potatoes, turnip, swede and globe artichokes steam beautifully in the pressure cooker.

My non-stick metal pudding basin is suitable for cooking all kinds of puddings.

Desserts such as crème caramel, cheesecake and bread and butter pudding can be even better when cooked in the pressure cooker. Because pressure cookers cook with steam, they excel at keeping desserts such as these moist and creamy. My pressure-cooked lemon cheesecake is wonderfully creamy, with a smoother, lighter texture than many conventionally cooked ones.

As with any new piece of cooking equipment, you'll need to use your pressure cooker a few times to feel comfortable with it. Once you've made a dish you like, try varying the ingredients to suit your own tastes or to make use of whatever might be in season. You'll soon gain the confidence to experiment with lots of different flavours.

What went wrong?

When you get used to this style of cooking, you'll find it much easier and simpler than conventional cooking. But for those just starting out, this list of solutions to common problems may be helpful.

I cooked a casserole in my pressure cooker and found the consistency was quite watery – I expected a thick, gravy-like sauce.

If there's too much liquid left after the specified cooking time, leave the lid off and simmer the ingredients on the stove for a few minutes until the sauce reaches the desired consistency. As each pressure cooker can differ in terms of the thickness of the base and the level of pressure involved, there'll be an element of trial and error in getting the liquid ratio right until you get used to your particular cooker.

My pudding/cake was not cooked through after the specified cooking time.

Most of the desserts in this book are cooked in a dish or tin placed inside the pressure cooker. The thickness of this cooking vessel will affect its ability to conduct heat, and so variations to the required cooking time may occur. I use a non-stick metal pudding basin with a lid (see opposite), which conducts heat effectively and is fantastic for cooking puddings. If you are using a ceramic or earthenware dish, you will need to increase the cooking time in my recipes by 10–15 minutes to get the same result. Also, the thickness of the base of your pressure cooker will be a factor in its ability to conduct heat, so again, trial and error is the answer.

The last time I made a stew in my pressure cooker, the meat and potatoes were cooked beautifully but the carrot chunks had fallen apart and were overcooked.

With this type of cooking, where all the ingredients are added together at the start of the process, it is important to make sure you cut ingredients to similar sizes and consistent thicknesses to ensure even cooking.

Having used my new cooker several times, I've noticed that the sides near the base have discoloured. How can I prevent this?

It's important that you never let the flames from the gas burner lick up around the sides of the pan. They are not made from the same 3-ply aluminium used for the base and will discolour if they come into contact with direct heat. Even when cooking on high heat, keep the flame low enough that it doesn't creep up the sides of the cooker, or switch to a smaller burner.

I recently cooked my favourite roast potatoes in the pressure cooker and this time I used the quick-release method as I was in a hurry to serve up. When I opened the lid I found the potatoes had crumbled and fallen apart.

Both the quick-release and cold-water release methods of releasing pressure can be harsh on some foods, and can cause meat to toughen and some soft vegetables to fall apart. It is preferable to use the natural-release method wherever possible, as it is gentler on food.

Nibbles & light meals

Hummus bi tahini

There's hardly any need to introduce this popular Lebanese spread, which is usually served with flatbread. I've given you the option of using soaked or unsoaked chickpeas, depending on whether or not you've planned ahead for this dish. I like to keep a jar of tahini, the paste made from ground sesame seeds, always on hand for making hummus.

Makes about 2 cups / Prep 15 mins / Cook 10 or 35 mins

1 cup dried chickpeas

juice of 2 lemons

2 cloves garlic, crushed

½ cup tahini

salt

a little olive oil, to garnish

ground cayenne or sweet paprika, to serve

toasted flatbread, to serve

1 If time allows, cover the chickpeas with cold water and soak overnight, then drain and rinse them.

2 Place the soaked or unsoaked chickpeas in the pressure cooker and add water to cover. Close the lid and lock it, then bring the cooker to low pressure over high heat. Once low pressure has been reached, reduce the heat to stabilise pressure. Cook on low for 10 minutes for soaked chickpeas or 35 minutes for unsoaked chickpeas.

3 Release the pressure using the natural-release method. Unlock the lid and check the chickpeas have softened enough to be blended – if not, give them another minute or two at low pressure. Drain the chickpeas in a colander, reserving 1 cup of the cooking liquid. Let the chickpeas cool slightly.

4 Set aside a few whole chickpeas to garnish the dish. Purée the rest in a blender or food processor, pouring in about a third of the lemon juice and enough of the reserved cooking liquid to make a smooth paste. Add the crushed garlic and some more lemon juice and process, gradually adding the tahini as you mix. Blend to a creamy paste, then add more lemon juice and salt to taste.

5 Spoon the hummus into a serving bowl and make a slight depression in the centre with the back of the spoon. Pour a little olive oil into the middle, garnish with the reserved chickpeas and sprinkle with the ground cayenne or paprika. Serve with plenty of toasted flatbread to scoop up the hummus.

✳ *If not using immediately, soaked chickpeas should be drained and kept in the refrigerator until ready to cook. Cooked chickpeas can be frozen in an airtight container and kept for up to 2 months. If you plan on freezing chickpeas, remove them from the heat a little before they are completely cooked, then finish the cooking process when you defrost them.*

Hummus bi tahini (left), White bean dip (back), Lentil tapenade canapés (front)

Lentil tapenade

Whether for a picnic, a quick snack or a light lunch, there is nothing nicer than a bowl of this delicious paste of lentils, olives and capers. Tapenade is all the better for being made ahead and stored in an airtight container in the refrigerator.

Capers are sold both in jars and loose, and my favourites are the tiny salted ones found at Italian delicatessens. These need to be thoroughly rinsed before using.

Makes about 2 cups / Prep 15 mins / Cook 10 mins

1 cup green lentils

2 cups Vegetable Stock (see page 39)

4 large cloves garlic, finely chopped

2 tablespoons sun-dried tomatoes, sliced

1 tablespoon olive oil

¼ cup capers

½ cup black olives, pitted and chopped

2 tablespoons lemon juice

salt and freshly ground black pepper

½ cup chopped flat-leaf parsley

crusty bread, toast or flatbread, to serve

1   Wash the lentils thoroughly and drain. Place in the pressure cooker with the stock, garlic and tomatoes. Close the lid and lock it, then bring the cooker to high pressure over high heat. Once high pressure has been reached, reduce the heat to stabilise pressure, and cook for 15 minutes.

2   Release the pressure using the natural-release method and remove the lid. Let the mixture cool for 5 minutes.

3   Transfer the lentil mixture to a blender or a food processor. Add the oil, capers, olives, lemon juice, and salt and pepper to taste, and process for about 20 seconds until a coarse paste has formed. Stir in the parsley and transfer the tapenade to a serving bowl. Serve with crusty bread, toast or flatbread.

*   *This tapenade also makes very smart little canapés. Try some dolloped on top of a slice each of tomato and bocconcini on some toasted flatbread. Or cut the bases off some large cherry tomatoes, scoop out the pulp and seeds carefully with a tiny teaspoon and invert the tomatoes, sprinkled lightly with salt, on paper towels. Drain for 30 minutes, then fill them with some tapenade, garnish with a tiny parsley leaf and arrange on a serving dish.*

White bean dip

If you love hummus but are trying to cut back a little on the kilojoules, this is the dip for you – the beans provide the same silkiness that the tahini would normally give. You can give this dip an Italian twist by adding a robust punch of rosemary (1 tablespoon chopped rosemary leaves) in place of the cumin.

When cooking with dried pulses, it's a good idea to wash up all your equipment straight away, before the bean paste dries and becomes difficult to budge.

Makes about 2 cups / Prep 10 mins / Cook 15 mins

1 cup dried white (cannellini, haricot
   or lima) beans

2 cloves garlic, peeled

1 green onion, roughly chopped

1 teaspoon ground cumin

½ teaspoon chilli powder (optional)

¼ cup olive oil

lemon juice, to taste

salt and freshly ground black pepper

crusty bread, toast or flatbread, to serve

1 Place the beans in a bowl and cover with cold water. Soak for several hours or overnight, then drain before use.

2 Put the soaked beans in the pressure cooker along with 2 cups water. Add the garlic, green onion, cumin and chilli, if using. Close the lid and lock it, then bring the cooker to high pressure over high heat. Once high pressure has been reached, reduce the heat to stabilise pressure and cook for 15 minutes. Release the pressure using the natural-release method and unlock the lid. Let the beans cool in the cooker then drain, reserving the cooking liquid.

3 Blend the beans, garlic and onion to a purée, adding sufficient reserved cooking liquid to make a thick dipping consistency. Finally, blend in the olive oil and lemon juice, and season to taste. Serve at room temperature with some crusty bread, toast or flatbread.

* *For a really special garnish, mix 2 tablespoons of extra virgin olive oil with a good pinch of chilli powder or paprika. Spoon the white bean dip into a shallow serving bowl and drizzle with the spiced oil. Alternatively spoon onto wedges of flatbread and drizzle with the oil. For a great alternative to plain flatbread, try this spiced version instead. Preheat your grill, and in a small bowl combine ¼ cup fresh mixed herbs (such as parsley, basil and oregano) and ¼ cup olive oil. Cut rounds of flatbread into wedges, place them on a baking tray and brush with the oil mixture. Cook under the hot grill until golden, turning once.*

Eggs & spinach in ramekins

These eggs are wonderfully soft and creamy, and delicious for a decadent breakfast or a light lunch. You can vary the flavourings depending on what you have to hand – a little diced ham or smoked salmon, some cooked mushrooms, some finely chopped herbs, a little goat's cheese or some diced feta would work well. You could even use the Peperonata on page 73 – just add a spoonful to each ramekin before adding the eggs.

If you haven't any ramekins you may like to consider investing in some small soufflé dishes, which come in very handy in the kitchen.

Serves 2–4 / Prep 5 mins / Cook 6 mins

15 g butter, plus extra for greasing

1 cup baby spinach leaves

1–2 tablespoons finely chopped green onions, white and pale-green parts only

4 baby roma or cherry tomatoes, diced

4 large eggs

⅓ cup cream

freshly ground black pepper

2 tablespoons freshly grated or shaved parmesan

hot buttered toast, to serve

1 Butter the insides of four small ramekins. Line the base of each dish with the spinach leaves, then add the green onions and the diced tomato, squashing them in slightly to leave a small indentation in the centre.

2 Break an egg into each ramekin and pour over the cream, then season with pepper and top with a knob of butter. Cover each ramekin tightly with a small piece of foil.

3 Pour 1½ cups water into the pressure cooker and put in the trivet. Arrange the ramekins on the trivet. Close the lid and lock it, then bring the cooker to high pressure over high heat. Once high pressure has been reached, reduce the heat to stabilise pressure and cook on high for 6 minutes. Release the pressure using the quick-release or cold-water release method, open the lid and, using oven mitts, carefully remove one of the ramekins. Lift the foil to check the egg is just set – if not, replace the lid, lock it and return to high pressure to cook for just a minute or so longer.

4 Top each egg with parmesan before serving immediately with hot buttered toast.

✷ *Silverbeet can be used in place of the baby spinach leaves but you'll need to cook it lightly first. Pop 1 cup of shredded silverbeet in the ramekins with a little butter and cook for 3 minutes on high pressure. Then add the rest of the ingredients and cook as above.*

Peppery carrot salad

This dish is of Moroccan origin and is wonderfully versatile. Serve it cold as a dip with flatbreads, as part of a mezze of small dishes, or as a salad along with barbecued meats; or warm as a vegetable side dish. It's even great in salad sandwiches.

Harissa, a North African condiment, is a thick and fiery hot chilli paste fragrant with spices and steeped in olive oil.

Serves 4–6 / Prep 10 mins / Cook 10 mins

4 large carrots, peeled and quartered

2 cloves garlic, peeled

salt and freshly ground black pepper

¼ cup extra virgin olive oil

1 tablespoon red- or white-wine vinegar

1 teaspoon harissa *or* a good pinch chilli powder

1 teaspoon sweet paprika

1 teaspoon ground cumin

1 teaspoon ground coriander

½ cup coriander leaves, torn

½ cup mint leaves, torn

toast, to serve

black olives, to garnish

1 Place the carrots and garlic in the pressure cooker along with 1 cup water and a little salt. Close the lid and lock it, then bring the cooker to high pressure over high heat. Once high pressure has been reached, reduce the heat to stabilise pressure, and cook for 10 minutes.

2 Release the pressure using the natural-release method. Drain the carrots and garlic and transfer to a bowl. Mash roughly with a fork then stir in the remaining ingredients. Season to taste, spoon onto toast, then garnish with the olives and serve.

Salmon bread soufflé

Light and tender, and very easy to make when you feel like something special, this bread soufflé can be varied in many ways (see suggestions below). If you want a little contrast in texture and a fresh look, you might like to top the soufflé with breadcrumbs, pan-fried in a little butter, just before serving. Serve a green salad alongside the soufflé to make this a complete meal.

Try making these in four 1-cup-capacity ramekins or soufflé dishes (as in the photo), covering each one tightly with foil, and they'll cook in 15 minutes.

Serves 4 / Prep 10 mins / Cook 20 mins

1 × 220 g can pink or red salmon

1½ cups fresh breadcrumbs

6 green onions, white and pale-green parts only, chopped

1 tablespoon lemon juice

2 tablespoons melted butter

salt and freshly ground black pepper

2 eggs, beaten

1½ cups hot milk

green salad, to serve

1 Butter a 5-cup-capacity soufflé dish.

2 Drain the salmon, removing any skin and bones, and lightly flake with a fork. Combine with the breadcrumbs, green onion, lemon juice and butter, and season to taste. Mix the eggs and hot milk together and fold into the salmon mixture.

3 Fill the soufflé dish with the salmon mixture and cover tightly with foil. Place a trivet or steamer insert into the pressure cooker, and add 1½ cups water. Place the soufflé dish on a folded tea towel or piece of muslin. Pick up the ends of the cloth, lift the dish then carefully lower it onto the trivet or steamer insert. Fold the ends of the cloth over the dish and leave there while it cooks.

4 Close the lid and lock it, then bring the cooker to low pressure over high heat. Once low pressure has been reached, reduce the heat to stabilise pressure, and cook for 25 minutes. Release the pressure using the natural-release method, unlock and remove the lid. Use tongs to pull out the ends of the cloth over the sides of the cooker to cool. After a few seconds, pick up the cloth ends and carefully use them to lift the dish from the cooker. Lift the foil and check the soufflé – it should be puffed up and just set. Serve immediately with a green salad.

✳ *You can substitute the salmon, green onion and lemon juice for any of the following to make delicious variations:*

Ham and asparagus: add ½ cup diced ham and some blanched asparagus spears, cut into short sections.

Smoked salmon: add 100–200 g diced smoked salmon and some freshly chopped flat-leaf parsley or chives.

Cheese: add ½ cup freshly grated parmesan and 1 cup freshly grated cheddar cheese.

Spicy beef chilli on warm burritos

This is very much a family dish and one that kids will love. Those who can tolerate heat might like to up the chilli content and use a whole chilli. Burritos and tortillas are available in most supermarkets or delicatessens and make a great store-cupboard standby for these sorts of meals.

Serves 4 / Prep 15 mins / Cook 15 mins

250 g lean minced beef

½ small white or brown onion, chopped

1 clove garlic, chopped

½ bird's eye chilli, deseeded and chopped

2 drops Tabasco sauce

½ teaspoon ground coriander

½ teaspoon ground cumin

¼ cup olive oil

1 tomato, finely diced

1 tablespoon freshly chopped coriander

salt and freshly ground black pepper

4 large, soft burritos

1 red capsicum, white insides and seeds removed, flesh cut into fine strips

few handfuls mixed salad leaves

coriander sprigs, to garnish

light sour cream, to serve

1   In a bowl, combine the beef, onion, garlic, chilli, Tabasco sauce and spices and mix thoroughly. Heat 2 tablespoons of olive oil in the pressure cooker, add the beef mixture and cook over a moderate heat for a few minutes, until the meat is lightly browned, stirring frequently to break up the lumps. Add the tomato, coriander and 2 tablespoons water and season to taste. Close the lid and lock it, then bring the cooker to low pressure over high heat. Once low pressure has been reached, reduce the heat to stabilise pressure and cook for 15 minutes. Release the pressure using the natural-release method and unlock the lid.

2   Meanwhile, warm the burritos in the microwave according to the instructions on the packet. Heat the remaining oil in a small frying pan and fry the capsicum strips over high heat for 5 minutes or until softened.

3   To serve, place a warmed burrito on each plate. Spoon some spicy beef mixture in the centre, then top with the capsicum strips and salad leaves. Roll the burritos up, cut them in half and serve garnished with coriander, and with a bowl of sour cream on the table for everyone to dollop on as they like.

Spicy eggplant & tomato

This a lovely eggplant dish to enjoy with rice, or as a side dish with a curry or Moroccan-style braise. I also like to stir in a little yoghurt and serve it as a dip with plain pappadams.

Serves 4 / Prep 15 mins / Cook 15 mins

1 tablespoon olive or rice bran oil

½ teaspoon cumin seeds

1–2 tablespoons finely chopped ginger

1 small white or brown onion, sliced

½ teaspoon ground turmeric

½ teaspoon chilli powder

1 teaspoon ground coriander

500 g tomatoes, chopped

2 eggplants, cut into chunks

1 teaspoon sugar

steamed rice, to serve

1 Heat the oil in the pressure cooker over medium heat. Add the cumin seeds and fry until they begin to spit, then add the ginger and onion. Cook for 2–3 minutes, until the onion is soft and golden. Stir in the spices and cook for 1 minute, until fragrant.

2 Add the tomatoes along with their juices and bring to a boil, then add the eggplant and sugar. Close the lid and lock it, then bring the cooker to high pressure over high heat. Once high pressure has been reached, reduce the heat to stabilise pressure and cook for 10 minutes. Release the pressure using the natural-release method and unlock and remove the lid. Let the mixture cool in the cooker for 5 minutes.

3 Transfer to a large dish and serve with steamed rice.

Terrine or pâté maison

This terrine is typical of the kind the French love. They pop small, thickish chunks on pieces of crusty bread ripped straight from baguettes. A small bowl of pickled cornichons (small, intensely sour pickled cucumbers), a handful of radishes and a glass of wine makes the meal complete. In France, these terrines are often bought in *charcuteries* but they are also regularly made at home. This one I've called *maison* because it can be varied, as it is in French homes, according to your preferences. The name terrine refers both to the container and the meat mixture baked in it.

Terrines are at their best a few days after making, so make this ahead of when you plan to serve it.

Serves 6–8 / Prep 20 mins / Cook 50 mins

2 tablespoons shelled pistachios

500 g minced pork *or* 250 g each minced pork and veal

300 g chicken livers, trimmed and finely chopped

1 small white onion, very finely chopped

1 clove garlic, crushed

¼ teaspoon ground white pepper

¼ teaspoon ground cloves

¼ teaspoon ground ginger

½ teaspoon grated nutmeg

1 tablespoon chopped flat-leaf parsley

2 sprigs fresh thyme, leaves picked

2 tablespoons brandy

2 teaspoons salt

1 thin slice pork fat (see note on page 28) *or* 6–8 rashers lightly smoked streaky bacon

1 or 2 small bay leaves

1 To blanch the pistachios, put the nuts into a small bowl, cover with boiling water and leave for 5 minutes. When cool enough to handle, the nuts will slip easily from their skins.

2 Place all the ingredients except the pork fat or bacon rashers and the bay leaves in a large mixing bowl, and mix well to thoroughly combine, preferably using your hands (you can wear thin disposable gloves if you like).

3 Choose a terrine that will fit into your pressure cooker and line it with the pork fat or bacon rashers, leaving the ends to hang over the edge. Firmly pack the meat mixture into the terrine and fold the overhanging fat or bacon over the top, then garnish with the bay leaves.

4 Cover tightly with a folded piece of foil, and a lid if you have one. Place a trivet in the pressure cooker and add 1½ cups water. Place the terrine on a folded tea towel or piece of muslin. Pick up the ends of the cloth, lift the terrine then carefully lower it onto the trivet. Fold the cloth ends over the terrine and leave there while it cooks. Close the lid and lock it, then bring the cooker to low

pressure over high heat. Once low pressure has been reached, reduce the heat to stabilise pressure and cook for 50 minutes. Release the pressure using the natural-release method and unlock and remove the lid.

5 Use tongs to pull out the ends of the cloth over the sides of the cooker to cool. After a few seconds, pick up the cloth ends and carefully use them to lift the terrine from the cooker. Remove the lid of the terrine, if it has one. Keeping the foil intact, place a light weight such as a small bag of rice on top and leave to cool. Once cool, place the terrine on a small tray and transfer to the refrigerator to chill. Keep for a day or two before serving to allow the flavours to develop. To serve, cut into slices.

* *The French use a special fresh pork fat to line the terrine and enclose the meat mixture. It gives the terrine a classic look and adds to its flavour. If you want to try this and don't mind the extra trouble, slice a long thinnish piece of fat from between the flesh and the rind of a piece of pork belly.*

Pork rillettes

This is a shredded pork pâté found in *charcuteries* throughout France. Little seasoning is used in the initial cooking, with the pork belly providing the fat (and plenty of flavour), then a grating of nutmeg is added to the shredded pork at the end before it is packed into pots. The best rillettes have an attractive rough texture. Serve this as you would any pâté, with crusty bread or toast, and pickled cornichons. Traditionally, the pork is slow-baked in the oven for four hours.

Makes 2 × 1½–2-cup pots / Prep 15 mins / Cook 1 hour

1.5 kg pork shoulder, cut into 8 cm chunks

500 g pork belly, cut into chunks

1 large clove garlic, peeled

few sprigs thyme

salt and freshly ground pepper

grated nutmeg, to taste

toast or fresh crusty bread, to serve

1 Place the pork chunks into the pressure cooker, rind side-up, with the garlic, thyme, salt and pepper. Add ¼ cup water, close the lid and lock it.

2 Bring the cooker to low pressure over high heat. Once low pressure has been reached, reduce the heat to stabilise pressure and cook for 1 hour. Release the pressure using the natural-release method and unlock and remove the lid. Check the pork – it should be very tender and soft enough to fall apart in shreds when pulled with a fork.

3 Lift the pieces of pork from the cooking liquid onto a chopping board. Cut away the rind and some of the excess fat. Using two forks, shred the meat finely, putting it into a bowl as it is done.

4 Strain the cooking liquid over the shredded pork and season with grated nutmeg and more salt if you like, tasting to check. Mix well, then pack the pork mixture tightly into small earthenware pots, making sure the surface is covered with the strained cooking liquid. Cover each pot with a small piece of foil and the lid if there is one. Refrigerate overnight to allow the flavours to develop, then serve with piping hot toast or fresh crusty bread.

Onion marmalade

I haven't met anyone who doesn't love soft, sticky, sweet and tangy onion marmalade.
Try it on your next steak sandwich, stir a spoonful or two into a gravy, serve it with roast beef,
use it to jazz up sausages or pop into a ploughman's lunch. I usually make mine with red
onions, though white or brown onions are good too.

Makes 2½ cups / Prep 15 mins / Cook 45 mins

75 g butter

1 kg red onions, thinly sliced

¼ cup red wine

¼ cup sugar

2 tablespoons balsamic vinegar

salt and freshly ground black pepper

1 Melt the butter in the pressure cooker over medium heat. Add the onions and cook on high heat, stirring until well coated with butter. Stir in the wine and sugar. Close the lid, lock it and bring the cooker to low pressure over high heat. Once low pressure has been reached, reduce the heat to stabilise pressure and cook for 15 minutes. Remove from the heat and release the pressure using the quick-release or cold-water release method.

2 Stir through the balsamic vinegar, then close the lid, lock it and bring to low pressure on high heat again. Once low pressure has been reached, reduce the heat to stabilise pressure and cook for a further 10 minutes.

3 Remove from the heat and release the pressure using the quick-release or cold-water release method, then return to the stove and simmer over high heat for a further 20 minutes until the liquid is thick and syrupy.

4 Season the onion marmalade with salt and pepper, leave to cool, then stir well and ladle into jars. Seal and refrigerate for up to 3 weeks.

Date & tamarind chutney (back), Onion marmalade (centre), Tomato & capsicum chutney (front)

Date & tamarind chutney

This is a chutney you could serve with a curry, but it's also good for adding a punch to everyday grills. Try it in a cheese sandwich – it's delicious.

Makes 2 cups / Prep 10 mins / Cook 10 mins

2 sticks cinnamon

5 cardamom pods, bruised

2 teaspoons whole cloves

500 g pitted dates

1 cup white-wine vinegar

½ cup firmly packed brown sugar

2 teaspoons salt

¼ cup peanut or rice bran oil

2 tablespoons tamarind concentrate

2 teaspoons chilli powder

1 Combine all the ingredients in the pressure cooker, mixing well. Close the lid, lock it and bring the cooker to low pressure over high heat. Once low pressure has been reached, reduce the heat to stabilise pressure and cook for 10 minutes. Release the pressure using the natural-release method and unlock and remove the lid.

2 Give the chutney a good stir before spooning into one large jar or two smaller ones. Seal and leave for a week or two before using.

Tomato & capsicum chutney

The men in my family in particular love to be able to grab a jar of chutney to spice up a grilled chop. This one is also good in sandwiches with cold meats. Cooking this on the stove would normally take 1½ hours, which becomes a little irritating when the smell of vinegar starts to penetrate throughout the house. The pressure cooker reduces the cooking time by half, and because the cooking smells are limited when cooking under pressure, those pervasive odours are reduced.

Makes 4–5 cups / Prep 15 mins / Cook 40–45 mins

1 kg ripe red tomatoes, chopped

2 onions, sliced

2 red capsicums, white insides and seeds removed, sliced

⅔ cup white-wine vinegar

1 cup brown sugar

2 tablespoons salt

grated rind of 1 lemon

grated rind of 1 orange

½ teaspoon freshly ground black pepper

1 teaspoon ground ginger

1 Combine everything in the pressure cooker, mixing well. Close the lid, lock it and bring the cooker to low pressure over high heat. Once low pressure has been reached, reduce the heat to stabilise pressure and cook for 20 minutes. Release the pressure using the natural-release method and unlock and remove the lid.

2 Return the chutney to the stove, letting it simmer, uncovered, over high heat for another 20–25 minutes until nicely thickened. Give it a stir every now and then.

3 Cool slightly then spoon into jars and seal. Leave for a week or two before using.

Stocks & soups

Stocks

Stock, or bouillon, is the clear, flavourful liquid that remains after meat, fish or vegetables have been simmered for some time in water. Done the traditional way, this can take hours; in a pressure cooker, it takes much less time.

Making stock is so simple. It's essential for making great soups, and it's also wonderful to have on hand in the freezer for making sauces and gravies or for adding to braises and casseroles. Stock made from beef is generally brown or golden in colour; poultry, veal and vegetables make a light golden or white stock, and fish a clear stock. Pressure-cooking not only helps to intensify the flavours of the meat and aromatics added to the stock, but because the temperature is higher in a pressure cooker than in a conventional pan, the collagen in bones and meat is converted into gelatine more quickly, doing away with the need for long, slow cooking.

Vegetable stock is a good all-rounder, especially as more and more people opt out of eating meat. Use in place of beef or chicken stock in soups, sauces and casseroles. A good fish stock makes all the difference to fish soups and chowders. Get into the habit of keeping raw prawn heads, shells, fish heads and fish trimmings until you have enough to make a batch of fish stock: just pack them in freezer bags and store them in the freezer for up to 2 months.

Some guidelines to help you make a good stock:

- Use cold, clean water to maximise the extraction of flavour.

- Don't fill the cooker more than half-full. It is better to add less liquid, not only to prevent the valve foaming, but also to give you a stronger-tasting stock, which you can dilute later if you wish.

- Always cook stock at low pressure, watching that it doesn't rise to high pressure – reduce the heat as necessary.

- Keep herbs and spices subtle to give a clear, fresh-tasting stock. You can add other flavourings later for specific dishes.

Chicken stock

Makes 5–6 cups / Prep 5 mins / Cook 20 mins

1 kg chicken parts (necks, wings, backs)

1 carrot, thickly sliced

1 white or brown onion, thickly sliced

2 teaspoons salt

1 teaspoon black peppercorns

bouquet garni of leaves from 2 sticks celery,
    2 sprigs parsley, 1 sprig thyme and 1 bay leaf,
    all tied together in a bundle with kitchen string

1 Place all the ingredients in the pressure cooker
and add 5–6 cups water (making sure the cooker
is not more than half-filled).

2 Close the lid and lock it, then bring the cooker
to low pressure over high heat. Once low pressure
has been reached, reduce the heat to stabilise
pressure and cook for 20 minutes.

3 Release the pressure using the natural-release
method, leave to cool then remove the lid and
strain the stock through a fine sieve. Store in the
refrigerator for up to 1 week, or freeze in batches
for later use for up to 2 months. Skim any surface
fat before using.

Beef stock

Makes 5–6 cups / Prep 30 mins / Cook 30 mins

1 kg beef bones (shank, marrow, rib bones,
    or a combination – ask your butcher to crack
    or saw the bones for you)

500 g chuck steak or shin of beef, cut into chunks

1 carrot, thickly sliced

1 white or brown onion, thickly sliced

2 teaspoons salt

1 teaspoon black peppercorns

bouquet garni of leaves from 2 sticks celery,
    2 sprigs parsley, 1 sprig thyme and 1 bay leaf,
    all tied together in a bundle with kitchen string

1 Remove any large pieces of meat from the bones
and cut into chunks. For a really rich brown stock,
preheat the oven to 190˚C, then place the bones,
meat and vegetables in a large baking dish and
roast for about 20 minutes, turning the meat and
vegetables occasionally.

2 Place all the ingredients in the pressure cooker,
then add 5–6 cups water (making sure the cooker
is not more than half-filled).

3 Close the lid and lock it, then bring the cooker
to low pressure over high heat. Once low pressure
has been reached, reduce the heat to stabilise
pressure and cook for 30 minutes.

4 Release the pressure using the natural-release
method, leave to cool then remove the lid and
strain the stock through a fine sieve. Store in the
refrigerator for up to 1 week, or freeze in batches
for later use for up to 2 months. Skim any surface
fat before using.

Vegetable stock

Makes 6–7 cups / Prep 10 mins / Cook 20 mins

1 leek, white part only, well washed and chopped

3 sticks celery, chopped

1 parsnip, peeled and chopped

1 white turnip, peeled and chopped

1 head lettuce, chopped

100 g mushrooms, sliced

1 × 3 cm piece ginger, finely chopped

12 black peppercorns

2 teaspoons salt

bouquet garni of leaves from 2 sticks celery,
    2 sprigs parsley, 1 sprig thyme and 1 bay leaf,
    all tied together in a bundle with kitchen string

1 Place all the ingredients in the pressure cooker and add 6 cups water (making sure the cooker is not more than half-filled).

2 Close the lid and lock it, then bring the cooker to low pressure over high heat. Once low pressure has been reached, reduce the heat to stabilise pressure and cook for 20 minutes.

3 Release the pressure using the natural-release method and leave the stock to cool. Remove the lid and strain the stock through a fine sieve, pressing the vegetables against the sides of the sieve to extract the juices, and then discard the solids. Store the stock in the refrigerator for up to 1 week, or freeze in batches for later use for up to 2 months.

Fish stock

Makes 6 cups / Prep 10 mins / Cook 15 mins

2 kg fish trimmings – bones, heads (without gills)
    and skin or shells of any white-fleshed fish
    or shellfish

1 cup white wine *or* the juice of 1 lemon plus water
    to make 1 cup

1 white or brown onion, thickly sliced

2 teaspoons salt

1 teaspoon black peppercorns

bouquet garni of leaves from 2 sticks celery,
    2 sprigs parsley, 1 sprig thyme and 1 bay leaf,
    all tied together in a bundle with kitchen string

1 Place all the ingredients in the pressure cooker and add 5 cups water (making sure the cooker is not more than half-filled).

2 Close the lid and lock it, then bring the cooker to low pressure over high heat. Once low pressure has been reached, reduce the heat to stabilise pressure and cook for 15 minutes.

3 Release the pressure using the natural-release method, leave to cool then remove the lid and strain the stock through a fine sieve. Store in the refrigerator for up to 1 week, or freeze in batches for later use for up to 2 months.

Velvet pea & zucchini soup

Velvet in English, *velouté* in French: this soup has a wonderful satiny smooth texture. Nutritionists are always telling us to include more vegetables in our diet, and it's easy with soups like this one, which can be whipped up in 15 minutes flat.

Serves 4–6 / Prep 10 mins / Cook 15 mins

1 tablespoon butter

5 green onions, chopped

1 white onion, finely chopped

4 large zucchini, diced

2 cups frozen peas

2 large potatoes

4 cups Chicken Stock (see page 38) or Vegetable Stock (see page 39)

½ teaspoon salt

freshly ground black pepper

¼ cup light cream, plus extra to serve (optional)

crusty bread, to serve

1 Melt the butter in the pressure cooker over medium heat, and cook the green onion, onion and zucchini for 3 minutes until soft but not coloured. Add the peas, potatoes, stock and salt.

2 Close the lid and lock it, then bring the cooker to low pressure over high heat. Once low pressure has been reached, reduce the heat to stabilise pressure and cook for 8 minutes. Release the pressure using the natural-release method, unlock and remove the lid.

3 Let the mixture cool slightly, then transfer to a food processor or blender (or use a hand-held blender) and purée until smooth. Return the soup to the cooker and reheat gently. Just before serving, check for seasoning and stir in the cream. Ladle into bowls, swirl a little extra cream into each and top with a grinding of black pepper. Serve with plenty of crusty bread.

Rocket & potato soup

If you like the peppery fresh taste of rocket, you'll like this soup – and it's good for you, too. This is a wonderfully versatile recipe, as sorrel or English spinach can be used in place of the rocket.

Serves 6 / Prep 10 mins / Cook 15 mins

2 tablespoons olive oil

2 brown onions, finely chopped

2 large cloves garlic, finely chopped

4 large desiree potatoes, peeled and
   cut into chunks

4–5 cups Chicken Stock (see page 38)

1 bunch rocket, stalks trimmed and discarded,
   leaves sliced into fine shreds

¼ teaspoon cayenne pepper, or to taste

salt and freshly ground pepper

1 Heat 1 tablespoon of the oil in the pressure cooker over a moderately low heat, then add the onion and cook, stirring, for 3 minutes until translucent. Add the remaining tablespoon of oil, the garlic and potatoes and cook over a low heat, stirring occasionally, for 2 minutes.

2 Pour in 4 cups of the chicken stock. Close the lid and lock it, then bring the cooker to low pressure over high heat. Once low pressure has been reached, reduce the heat to stabilise pressure and cook for 8 minutes.

3 Release the pressure using the natural-release method, and unlock and remove the lid, leaving the soup to cool slightly for 5 minutes. Use a hand-held blender or food processor to purée the soup in batches then return to the cooker. Stir the shredded rocket into the soup, adding a little extra stock if needed to reach the desired consistency. Reheat the soup gently, add the cayenne pepper and salt and pepper to taste, and serve piping hot.

French onion soup

French onion soup should be thick with onions, and although it is usually made with beef stock, sometimes just water is used. It's very filling and can be served as a meal, or in a small bowl as a first course.

Serves 6 / Prep 15 mins / Cook 20 mins

45 g butter

1 tablespoon rice bran oil or olive oil

5 large onions (about 1 kg), thinly sliced

1 teaspoon salt

1 tablespoon plain flour

4 cups Beef Stock (see page 38) or water

½ cup dry white wine

freshly ground black pepper

1 large baguette, cut into 2.5 cm slices

2 cloves garlic, peeled and cut in half (optional)

1 Melt the butter and oil in the pressure cooker over medium heat. Add the onions and cook for about 8 minutes until softened and golden, stirring frequently (do not let them get too brown or burn, or the soup will become bitter). Sprinkle with salt and stir in the flour until well combined, then cook over medium heat for 2 minutes. Stir in the stock or water and the wine and season well with pepper.

2 Close the lid and lock it, then bring the cooker to low pressure over high heat. Once low pressure has been reached, reduce the heat to stabilise pressure and cook for 10 minutes. Release the pressure using the natural-release method, and unlock and remove the lid.

3 Meanwhile, toast the baguette slices until they are crisp and lightly coloured. Rub each bread slice with a cut garlic clove, if using, and serve alongside the soup.

✱ *For a more substantial meal in the cold weather, try soupe a l'oignon gratinée (pictured left). Place the toasted baguette slices into an ovenproof soup tureen or individual bowls, then pour the French onion soup over them. Top with plenty of freshly grated gruyère or emmental cheese, and place under a hot grill until the cheese melts and is lightly browned and bubbling. Serve hot with some fresh baguette alongside.*

Spinach, lemon & lentil soup

This is one of my favourite soups, first made for me by a charming Italian *nonna* in Melbourne. Not only is it the ultimate comfort food, but it's also wonderfully nourishing – with every spoonful you can feel it doing you good.

Serves 4 / Prep 15 mins / Cook 25 mins

250 g green lentils

1 bunch English spinach

1 tablespoon olive oil

1 leek, well washed and finely sliced

2 cloves garlic, crushed

3 potatoes, chopped

2 carrots, sliced

1 bay leaf

4 sprigs thyme

4 cups Vegetable Stock (see page 39)

⅓ cup lemon juice

salt and freshly ground black pepper

extra virgin olive oil, for drizzling

shaved parmesan, to garnish

lemon wedges, to serve

1 Place the lentils in a bowl, cover with cold water and leave to soak while you prepare the remaining ingredients. Wash the spinach thoroughly, trim and shred finely then set aside.

2 Heat the oil in the pressure cooker over medium heat. Add the leek and garlic and cook for 5 minutes, or until soft and golden. Then add the potato, carrot, bay leaf, thyme, stock, 2 cups water and the drained lentils to the cooker.

3 Close the lid and lock it, then bring the cooker to high pressure over high heat. Once high pressure has been reached, reduce the heat to stabilise pressure and cook for 20 minutes. Release the pressure using the natural-release method, and unlock and remove the lid. Carefully remove the bay leaf and thyme sprigs, then add the spinach and lemon juice and cook, uncovered, for 2 minutes, until the spinach is wilted.

4 Taste for seasoning, adding more salt and pepper if required. Ladle the soup into bowls and drizzle with a little extra virgin olive oil. Top with some shaved parmesan and serve with lemon wedges.

Summer beetroot soup

This bright pink soup can be delicious and wonderfully refreshing on a hot day, or comforting and nutritious on a cool day. Sour cream or natural yoghurt can be added as an alternative to buttermilk, and this makes the soup a deep red rather than a pretty pink. This dish looks dramatic garnished with dill, chives and natural yoghurt.

Serves 6 / Prep 20 mins / Cook 15 mins

3 large raw beetroot

3 cups Chicken Stock (see page 38)

2 Lebanese cucumbers, peeled and diced

2 tablespoons chopped chives, plus extra to garnish

2 tablespoons chopped dill, plus extra to garnish

salt and freshly ground black pepper

1 cup buttermilk, light sour cream or natural yoghurt

1 Wash the beetroot and place on the trivet in the pressure cooker. Pour in 1 cup water, close and lock the lid, then bring the cooker to high pressure over high heat. Once high pressure has been reached, reduce the heat to stabilise pressure and cook the beetroot for 15 minutes.

2 Release the pressure using the natural-release method, and unlock and remove the lid. Carefully lift out the beetroot with some tongs and, when they're cool enough to handle, slip the skins off with your fingers (wear some plastic, disposable gloves to prevent the beetroot staining your skin).

3 Roughly chop two of the beetroot and purée with the chicken stock in a blender (you can add more chicken stock if you would like a thinner consistency). Dice the remaining beetroot.

4 In a large bowl, combine the beetroot soup with the diced beetroot, cucumber, chives and dill. Stir well and chill until ready to serve.

5 Season to taste, then stir in the buttermilk or three-quarters of the sour cream or yoghurt. Have some soup bowls chilled and ready, then place an ice cube or two in each. Ladle in the soup and garnish with the remaining sour cream or yoghurt, some dill and chives.

✻ *You can also serve this soup hot — just heat the beetroot soup with the diced beetroot, then garnish with some cucumber, dill and chives.*

Portuguese fish soup

This thick broth makes for a filling soup or a light stew. The fish is added towards the end to prevent it becoming overcooked.

Serves 4–6 / Prep 15 mins / Cook 15 mins

2 tablespoons olive oil

4 cloves garlic, chopped

1 white onion, chopped

2 tomatoes, cut into large dice

good pinch saffron threads

3 potatoes, cut into small chunks

½ cup basmati rice

6 cups water *or* 3 cups Fish Stock (see page 39) and 3 cups water

salt and freshly ground black pepper

1 kg firm-fleshed fish such as barramundi, ling or flathead, skinned and cut into large chunks

extra virgin olive oil for serving

1 bunch coriander, washed, stems and leaves finely chopped

1 Put the olive oil, garlic, onion, tomato, saffron, potato, rice and water (or water and fish stock) into the pressure cooker and season with salt and pepper. Close and lock the lid, then bring the cooker to low pressure over high heat. Once low pressure has been reached, reduce the heat to stabilise pressure and cook for 8 minutes.

2 Release the pressure using the natural-release method, unlock and remove the lid, and add the fish pieces. Return the cooker to the heat and simmer, uncovered, for 3–4 minutes, until the fish is cooked through. Check for seasoning, adding more salt and pepper if necessary.

3 Ladle the soup into bowls and drizzle each serving with a little extra virgin olive oil. Sprinkle with chopped coriander and serve.

Scotch broth

This is one of the most welcome soups of winter – it's almost a meal in itself with a nice chunk of crusty bread. Find out if your butcher sells lamb neck chops, as they are fantastic in this soup.

Serves 8 / Prep 10 mins / Cook 25 mins

500 g lamb neck chops *or* 3–4 lamb shanks

¼ cup pearl barley

1–2 sticks celery, diced

1 carrot, sliced

1 leek, well washed and sliced

1 turnip, peeled and diced

1 white or brown onion, chopped

salt

¼ cup chopped flat-leaf parsley

1 Place the chops or shanks, pearl barley and vegetables in the pressure cooker, along with 5 cups water and salt to taste.

2 Close and lock the lid, then bring the cooker to low pressure over high heat. Once low pressure has been reached, reduce the heat to stabilise pressure and cook for 20 minutes. Release the pressure using the natural-release method, unlock and remove the lid. Let the mixture cool for 5 minutes or so.

3 Carefully lift the chops or shanks out onto a plate. When cool enough to handle, cut the meat away from the bones. Removing any fat and gristle, cut the meat into small pieces and return to the broth.

4 Reheat the broth gently, uncovered, adding a little more water if the soup is too thick. Stir in the chopped parsley and serve piping hot.

Split pea & ham soup

This is one of those throw-it-all-in-the-pot soups that end up being surprisingly delicious, nutritious and filling. No stock is necessary because a ham hock is used, which produces its own flavourful stock. I prefer to use less rather than more water during cooking, adding more liquid later if needed to reach the right consistency. If you have a lot leftover, this soup keeps well in the freezer for up to 1 month.

Serves 8 / Prep 15 mins / Cook 15 mins

500 g dried yellow or green split peas, rinsed

1 smoked ham hock

3 slices ginger

1 clove garlic, finely chopped

3 carrots, chopped

1 onion, chopped

2 teaspoons ground turmeric

1 teaspoon chilli powder

1–2 tablespoons lemon juice

salt and freshly ground black pepper

2 tablespoons chopped coriander
   or flat-leaf parsley

a few coriander leaves or some thinly sliced lemon,
   to garnish (optional)

1 Place the split peas in a bowl and cover with cold water. Soak for several hours or overnight, then drain before use.

2 Place the ham hock, soaked split peas, ginger, garlic, carrot, onion, turmeric and chilli powder in the pressure cooker, along with 6 cups water. Close the lid and lock it, then bring the cooker to high pressure over high heat. Once high pressure has been reached, reduce the heat to stabilise pressure and cook for 15 minutes.

3 Release the pressure using the natural-release method, unlock and remove the lid then carefully transfer the ham hock with a slotted spoon to a chopping board. Remove the meat from the bones, discarding the skin and fat, and cut into small dice. Add the diced ham to the soup, as well as the lemon juice, salt and freshly ground pepper to taste (at this point you can also add some hot water if you like, to reach the desired consistency).

4 Stir in the chopped coriander or parsley, then ladle the soup into warmed bowls and garnish with the coriander leaves or lemon slices, if using.

Vegetables

Pressure-roasted potatoes

This is now my favourite way of cooking potatoes. The flavour becomes wonderfully intense, and the texture soft and creamy. Have a go at the variations – you'll probably come up with some more once you get started.

Serves 4–6 / Prep 5 mins / Cook 15 mins

2 tablespoons rice bran oil or olive oil

3 large waxy potatoes, cut into quarters

1 tablespoon chopped flat-leaf parsley

2 teaspoons chopped thyme leaves

salt

1 Heat the oil in the pressure cooker over medium heat. Add the potatoes and fry for 5 minutes, turning until browned on all sides.

2 Remove the cooker from the heat, add the herbs, ¼ cup water and salt to taste. Quickly close the lid and lock it, then bring the cooker to high pressure over high heat. Once high pressure has been reached, reduce the heat to stabilise pressure and cook for 6 minutes. Release the pressure using the natural-release method and remove the lid. Serve the potatoes piping hot.

✱ *Try varying the flavours:*

Italian-style: throw some sliced garlic and rosemary leaves in with the potatoes about halfway through the frying time (and leave out the parsley and thyme).

Greek-style: add some oregano leaves instead of the parsley and thyme, and instead of ¼ cup water, use a mix of half lemon juice, half water.

Spanish-style: add some sliced garlic and a little paprika to the pan halfway through the frying time, and substitute the parsley and thyme with ½ cup coriander. Stir 1 tablespoon of tomato paste into the water before adding it to the cooker.

Braised artichokes with breadcrumb stuffing

I was lucky enough to discover the joys of this delectable vegetable early in life. I soon learnt that to partake of the beautiful heart of the artichoke, I had to start with the tougher outer leaves, pulling them through my teeth to strip off the flesh. Troublesome to eat, maybe, but enormous fun, especially when shared with good friends.

Serves 6 / Prep 15 mins / Cook 15 mins

1 tomato

6–8 globe artichokes

1 lemon, cut in half

1 cup breadcrumbs

½ cup freshly grated parmesan

¼ cup freshly chopped mixed herbs, such as parsley, oregano and mint

salt and freshly ground black pepper

¼ cup olive oil

½ cup white wine or water

1 white or brown onion, chopped

1 If you want to peel the tomato, drop it into boiling water for 10 seconds, then transfer it to cold water to cool. Use a small sharp knife to cut the skin around the calyx, then peel the skin away. Roughly chop the flesh and set aside.

2 To prepare the artichokes, remove the tough, outer leaves then cut one-third off the top of the artichoke with a sharp knife. Trim the stalks to 5 cm. As each artichoke is prepared, rub the surfaces with a cut lemon to prevent discolouring.

3 In a bowl, combine the breadcrumbs, cheese and herbs, add salt and pepper to taste, and moisten with 1 tablespoon of the olive oil. Open the leaves of the artichokes slightly and fill the spaces with the stuffing, pushing it well down into the base of the leaves. Drizzle in a little olive oil to seal.

4 Stand the artichokes upright in the pressure cooker, closely packed so they prop each other up. Pour in the white wine or water and add the remaining olive oil, the chopped onion and tomato. Close the lid and lock it, then bring the cooker to high pressure over high heat. Once high pressure has been reached, reduce the heat to stabilise pressure and cook for 15 minutes.

5 Release the pressure using the natural-release method and remove the lid. To serve, arrange the artichokes in a dish and spoon over some of the cooking juices.

* *To eat artichokes, remove the leaves one by one and pull the base of each leaf between clenched teeth to loosen the flesh. Work your way to the heart and enjoy its sweet tenderness. Provide finger bowls of warm water with slices of lemon for your guests to clean their fingers.*

Potato & pea curry

Serve this with Aromatic Rice Pilaf (see page 83), along with some pappadams and chutney, for an excellent light vegetarian meal.

Serves 4–6 / Prep 10 mins / Cook 10 mins

¼ cup peanut or rice bran oil

2 white onions, sliced

1 teaspoon cumin seeds

1 teaspoon ground turmeric

½ teaspoon chilli powder

2 cloves garlic, chopped

½ teaspoon grated ginger

¼ cup tomato paste

3 large potatoes, peeled and quartered

2 cups frozen peas, thawed

salt

½ cup boiling water

1 teaspoon garam masala

¼ cup freshly chopped coriander

pappadams, to serve

1 Heat the oil in the pressure cooker over medium heat then fry the onion and cumin seeds for 2 minutes until golden. Stir in the turmeric, chilli powder, garlic and ginger and cook for 10 seconds, then add the tomato paste, potatoes and peas. Stir well and season to taste with salt.

2 Add the boiling water then close the lid and lock it. Bring the cooker to low pressure over high heat. Once low pressure has been reached, reduce the heat to stabilise pressure and cook for 6 minutes. Release the pressure using the natural-release method, unlock and remove the lid. Sprinkle with the garam masala and coriander and serve with pappadams.

✱ *I also like to make this using 3 cups of cauliflower florets in place of the peas.*

Braised zucchini, beans & tomatoes

If you love vegetables lightly cooked with a natural fresh flavour, this is the dish for you.

Serves 6 / Prep 10 mins / Cook 5 mins

2 tablespoons olive oil

1 clove garlic, crushed

3 large zucchini, cut into chunks

5 pattypan or button squash, cut in half

300 g green beans, cut into thirds

salt and freshly ground black pepper

¼ cup chopped flat-leaf parsley

1 teaspoon freshly chopped thyme or oregano

1 punnet cherry tomatoes

1 Heat the oil in the pressure cooker over medium heat. Add the garlic, zucchini, squash and beans and cook for about 2 minutes, stirring frequently. Take care not to let the garlic burn.

2 Season well with salt and pepper and add the herbs, tomatoes and 2 tablespoons water. Close the lid and lock it, then bring the cooker to low pressure over high heat. Once low pressure has been reached, reduce the heat to stabilise pressure and cook for 3 minutes. Release the pressure using the natural-release method, unlock and remove the lid. Serve immediately.

Eggplant with tomato, raisins & feta

An unusual combination that works like a dream, and usually has vegetarians and meat-eaters alike requesting a second helping. This dish is even more delicious eaten the day after cooking.

Serves 4–6 / Prep 15 mins / Cook 15 mins

2 tablespoons olive oil

1 onion, chopped

3 cloves garlic, crushed

2 teaspoons ground coriander seeds, lightly toasted

1 teaspoon ground sweet paprika

1 × 400 g can diced tomatoes

2 tablespoons pine nuts, toasted

¼ cup raisins

2 eggplants, quartered lengthways with stem attached *or* 8 finger eggplants

salt and freshly ground black pepper

50–100 g feta cheese, crumbled, to serve

whole fresh mint leaves, to serve

1 Heat the oil in a pressure cooker over medium heat. Cook the onion for 5 minutes, until soft. Add the garlic and spices and cook another 2–3 minutes, until the spices are fragrant. Add the tomato, pine nuts and raisins and bring to a boil.

2 If using finger eggplants, prick the skin with a fork a few times. Lay the whole eggplant or eggplant quarters over the mixture and season well. Close the lid and lock it, then bring the cooker to low pressure over high heat. Once low pressure has been reached, reduce the heat to stabilise pressure and cook for 7 minutes.

3 Release the pressure using the natural-release method and remove the lid. The eggplants should be very tender – if not, give them another minute or so at low pressure. Serve warm or at room temperature on a large platter topped with the crumbled feta and mint leaves.

Cabbage with pancetta, garlic & rosemary

In this Italian-inspired recipe the cabbage is usually served al dente, which gives it quite a different flavour: fresher and much sweeter. But if you prefer your cabbage tender, leave it in for a bit longer (10 minutes in total) – cooked in the pressure cooker, it won't fill your kitchen with an unpleasant smell, as traditionally boiled cabbage can.

The best variety to use for this is Savoy cabbage, for its tender, crinkly leaf and sweeter flavour.

Serves 6–8 / Prep 5 mins / Cook 6–10 mins

100 g pancetta, cut into thin strips

1 clove garlic, finely chopped

good pinch rosemary leaves

1 tablespoon olive oil

1 kg cabbage, coarsely shredded

¼ cup Chicken Stock (see page 38) or white wine

freshly ground black pepper

1 Mix together the pancetta, garlic and rosemary. Heat the oil in the pressure cooker over low heat and gently fry the pancetta mixture for about 1 minute, until aromatic and sizzling. Add the shredded cabbage and toss to coat well, then add the stock or wine and season with pepper.

2 Close the lid and lock it, then bring the cooker to high pressure over high heat. Once high pressure has been reached, reduce the heat to stabilise pressure and cook for 6–10 minutes. Release the pressure using the natural-release method, unlock and remove the lid and serve immediately.

✱ *You can use bacon rashers in place of pancetta.*

Malaysian vegetable curry

Serve this delicious curry with steamed rice or with the coconut rice from
the Nasi Lemak recipe on page 97.

Serves 4 / Prep 15 mins / Cook 10 mins

1 stalk lemongrass

2 tablespoons vegetable oil

1 white or brown onion, finely chopped

1 clove garlic, peeled

2 tablespoons curry powder

½ teaspoon chilli powder

600 g vegetables (beans, zucchini, carrot, pumpkin, etc.),
   cut into small pieces

2 potatoes, cut into small chunks

1 teaspoon salt

1 × 270 ml can coconut milk

steamed rice, to serve

1 Use the back of a heavy chopping knife to bash along the length of the lemongrass stalk to soften
it, then tie it into a knot. Heat the oil in the pressure cooker over medium heat, then add the onion,
garlic and lemongrass and fry for 3–4 minutes, stirring often (take care not to let the garlic burn).
Add the curry and chilli powders and ¼ cup water and stir well until combined. Add the vegetables,
potatoes, salt and another ¼ cup water and mix well.

2 Close the lid and lock it, then bring the cooker to low pressure over medium heat. Once low
pressure has been reached, reduce the heat to stabilise pressure and cook for 5 minutes. Release
the pressure using the natural-release method, unlock and remove the lid. Stir in the coconut milk
and heat through, uncovered, over low heat for a minute or two before serving with steamed rice.

Peperonata

Serve this lovely Italian dish of peppers with plenty of crusty bread for a light meal, as an antipasto, a base for Eggs & Spinach in Ramekins (see page 17) or an omelette filling, or with fish, chicken or meat as a delicious vegetable dish.

Since no liquid is added to this dish, you'll need to bring it to pressure over medium rather than high heat to prevent the pan from scorching before the vegetables release their juices.

Serves 4–6 / Prep 10 mins / Cook 15 mins

2 tablespoons olive oil

1 white or brown onion, finely chopped

1 stick celery, finely sliced

3 large red capsicums, white insides and seeds removed, flesh cut into thin strips

1 clove garlic, finely chopped

250 g cherry tomatoes, halved

8 basil leaves, shredded

salt and freshly ground black pepper

crusty bread, to serve

1 Heat the oil in the pressure cooker over medium heat and fry the onion and celery for 3 minutes until soft. Toss through the capsicum, garlic, tomatoes and basil. Close the lid and lock it, then bring the cooker to low pressure over medium heat. Once low pressure has been reached, reduce the heat to stabilise pressure and cook for 10 minutes.

2 Release the pressure using the natural-release method, unlock and remove the lid. Season with salt and pepper and serve warm or at room temperature with plenty of crusty bread.

Potatoes braised with tomatoes & oregano

This is as good as potatoes get. There's no frying required, and the result is delicious, with slices of potatoes glistening in a lovely syrupy tomato sauce.

Serves 4 / Prep 10 mins / Cook 10 mins

5 potatoes, peeled and sliced 1 cm thick

3 tomatoes, sliced

1 large white or brown onion, sliced

1 clove garlic, crushed

1 teaspoon dried oregano

1 teaspoon allspice or paprika

2 tablespoons olive oil

1 teaspoon salt

1 Place all the ingredients in the pressure cooker with 2 tablespoons water and gently stir to mix. Close the lid and lock it, then bring the cooker to low pressure over medium heat. Once low pressure has been reached, reduce the heat to stabilise pressure and cook for 10 minutes.

2 Release the pressure using the natural-release method, unlock and remove the lid, and serve.

＊ *You can vary this in the following ways: use a punnet of cherry tomatoes, halved, in place of the sliced tomatoes; add 1 red capsicum, white insides and seeds removed, flesh cut into strips, to the mixture; toss through ¼ cup small black olives at the end; or toss through 1 tablespoon capers at the end. For a more substantial meal, brown some chicken pieces in the olive oil at the beginning, then add the remaining ingredients and continue with the recipe.*

Gypsy vegetable stew

This is a ratatouille of sorts, made from Mediterranean-style vegetables. It's delicious served warm or cold with a generous chunk of bread as a first course, or you can have it as an accompaniment to grilled or roasted meat. It keeps for several days in the fridge, so it's a useful dish to have on hand.

Serves 4–6 / Prep 15 mins / Cook 5 mins

2 white or brown onions, sliced

2 green or red capsicums, halved, white insides and seeds removed

3 zucchini, cut into chunks

2–3 cloves garlic, roughly chopped

1 eggplant, cut into chunks

2 tomatoes, cut into chunks

1 × 400 g can diced tomatoes
  or 1 punnet cherry tomatoes

salt and freshly ground black pepper

⅓ cup olive oil

juice of 1 lemon

1 Arrange in the pressure cooker, in separate layers, first the onions, then the capsicum, zucchini, garlic and eggplant, and lastly the fresh and canned or cherry tomatoes, sprinkling each layer with salt and pepper. Pour the oil and lemon juice over the vegetables.

2 Close the lid and lock it, then bring the cooker to low pressure over high heat. Once low pressure has been reached, reduce the heat to stabilise pressure and cook for 5 minutes.

3 Release the pressure using the natural-release method and remove the lid. Serve warm or at room temperature.

✻ *Recently, when buying vegetables for this dish, I discovered baby purple and white eggplants (some smaller than a golf ball), baby green onions, bright-red small capsicum and small egg tomatoes. The vegetables were so young and tender that I cooked them all whole (apart from the capsicums, which I quartered), and they were delicious. It's a reminder that you can always adapt your cooking to suit whatever is fresh and in season at the time.*

Grains & pulses

Steamed rice

basmati, jasmine or brown rice

good pinch of salt

water

1 Place the rice in the pressure cooker and add salt and water. Close the lid and lock it, then bring the cooker to low pressure over high heat. Once low pressure has been reached, reduce the heat to stabilise pressure and cook for 6 minutes for basmati or jasmine rice, or 15–18 minutes for brown rice.

2 Release the pressure using the natural-release method, unlock and remove the lid, and serve.

Type of rice	Amount	Amount of water	Cooking time in minutes	Pressure level	Release
Jasmine rice	1 cup	1½ cups	6	Low	Natural
Basmati rice	1 cup	1½ cups	6	Low	Natural
Brown rice	1 cup	1½ cups	15–18	Low	Natural
Arborio, carnaroli or vialone rice	1½ cups	5½–6 cups	6	High	Natural

Steamed cardamom rice

Serves 4 / Prep 5 mins / Cook 6 or 15–18 mins

1½ cups basmati or brown rice

60 g butter

1 cup Chicken Stock (see page 38)

1 teaspoon salt

6 whole cardamom pods

1 stick cinnamon

4 cloves

1 Wash the rice under cold running water and drain well. Melt the butter in the pressure cooker, add the rice and stir over medium heat for 3 minutes. Add the stock, salt, cardamom, cinnamon, cloves and 1¼ cups water.

2 Close the lid and lock it, then bring the cooker to low pressure over high heat. Once low pressure has been reached, reduce the heat to stabilise pressure and cook for 6 minutes for basmati, or 15–18 minutes for brown rice. Release the pressure using the natural-release method, unlock and remove the lid. Fluff the rice with a fork, and serve with curried eggs, grilled chicken or other grilled meats.

Aromatic rice pilaf

This is a delicious way to cook rice; the grains absorb the liquid and become plump and flavoursome. It's a nutritious meal in itself, simply eaten with yoghurt, a chutney or pickle and even pappadams, if you like.

Serves 4 / Prep 10 mins / Cook 10 mins

2 tablespoons olive oil

1 white or brown onion, finely chopped

1 teaspoon ground cumin

1 teaspoon ground coriander

½ teaspoon ground turmeric

2 tablespoons sultanas (optional)

1½ cups basmati rice

2¼ cups Chicken Stock (see page 38) or water

salt

100 g baby spinach leaves

Greek-style yoghurt, to serve

1 Heat the oil in the pressure cooker over medium heat, and gently fry the onion until soft and golden. Stir in the spices and sultanas and cook until fragrant. Add the rice and cook, stirring, for a few minutes. Add the stock or water and season to taste with salt. Close the lid and lock it, then bring the cooker to low pressure over high heat. Once low pressure has been reached, reduce the heat to stabilise pressure and cook for 6 minutes.

2 Release the pressure using the natural-release method, unlock and remove the lid. Fold through the baby spinach and serve with a dollop of yoghurt.

Risotto bianco

When made with good Italian risotto rice and homemade chicken stock, this creamy, luxurious rice dish from northern Italy is the food of the gods. It can be as simple as rice, stock and parmesan, or it can be richly studded with seafood, chicken, mushrooms or other vegetables. Traditionally the liquid is added slowly and the rice is stirred constantly, with the cook devoting at least 15 minutes to standing at the stove. The pressure-cooker method takes half the time, but still results in creamy rice, with each grain separate and still firm to the bite, that won't disappoint risotto devotees. The perfect risotto should have the consistency of creamy porridge or a thick soup. The cheese is added at the end of cooking.

For this dish, you'll get the best results from a stainless steel cooker with a thick 3-ply base.

Serves 4–6 / Prep 10 mins / Cook 15 mins

30 g butter, plus a little extra if you like

1 small white or brown onion, finely chopped

1½ cups arborio, carnaroli or vialone rice

½ cup dry white wine

5½ cups Chicken Stock (see page 38)

salt and freshly ground black pepper

2 tablespoons freshly grated parmesan, plus extra to garnish

1 Melt the butter in the pressure cooker and fry the onion over low heat for a few minutes until golden. Add the rice and stir until glistening.

2 Stir in the wine, then add the chicken stock and season well. Close the lid and lock it, then bring the cooker to high pressure over high heat. Once high pressure has been reached, reduce the heat to stabilise pressure and cook for 6 minutes.

3 Release the pressure using the natural-release method, unlock and remove the lid. The rice should be al dente, but with a nice creamy texture. Return the lid to the cooker and leave the risotto to stand off the heat for a few minutes to allow the liquid to be fully absorbed. Gently fold through the cheese and extra butter, if using. Season well and serve with extra grated parmesan on top.

✱ *The variations on this basic risotto are almost limitless. For simple variations, try adding roasted pumpkin or sweet potato, sautéed zucchini, cooked chicken or some cooked seafood to the rice just before you stir the cheese through. Or you could try:*

Risotto Milanese: Add a good pinch of saffron threads to Risotto Bianco when stirring in the wine.

Mushroom risotto: Sauté 2 cups of small sliced mushrooms in a little butter and add to the Risotto Bianco at the end of cooking. A teaspoon of truffle oil can be added to finish.

Tomato and basil risotto: Take a punnet of cherry tomatoes, cut them in half and sauté them in a little butter until softened. Fold through the risotto bianco at the end with a few torn basil leaves.

Asparagus risotto (pictured right): Cut asparagus spears into 3 cm pieces and cook in some simmering chicken stock for 3 minutes or until tender, and add to the risotto at the end.

Barley risotto with chorizo & mushrooms

Have a play with this great recipe – you can use sliced leek instead of onion, or add roasted cherry tomatoes in place of the mushrooms and chorizo.

Serves 4–6 / Prep 15 mins / Cook 20 mins

50 g butter

1 white or brown onion, finely chopped

2 cloves garlic, crushed

200 g chorizo, thinly sliced on the diagonal

1¾ cups pearl barley

5 cups Chicken Stock (see page 38)

salt and freshly ground black pepper

250 g button mushrooms, quartered

⅓ cup freshly chopped flat-leaf parsley

½ cup freshly grated parmesan

shaved parmesan, to serve

1 Melt half of the butter in the pressure cooker over medium heat. Sauté the onion, garlic and three-quarters of the chorizo for 4 minutes, until the chorizo is nicely browned.

2 Add the barley and stock and season well with salt and pepper. Close the lid and lock it, then bring the cooker to high pressure over high heat. Once high pressure has been reached, reduce the heat to stabilise pressure and cook for 15 minutes. Release the pressure using the natural-release method, unlock and remove the lid. The barley should be tender but still have a little bite to it and, though most of the liquid is absorbed, should have a slightly soupy consistency.

3 Meanwhile, preheat a grill on high. Place the remaining chorizo on a baking tray and grill for 2 minutes until golden and crisp. Drain on paper towel and set aside. Melt the remaining butter in a large frying pan, and fry the mushrooms for 5 minutes on high heat, until golden.

4 Fold the mushrooms, parsley and parmesan through the barley and season to taste. Top with the grilled chorizo and some shaved parmesan to serve.

Chickpea curry

Dried beans and peas will not soften easily once an acidulant like tomato is added. The addition of salt also inhibits their cooking. That's why it is important to use chickpeas that are already cooked for this recipe.

Serves 6 / Prep 15 mins / Cook 20 mins

2 tablespoons olive oil

1 tablespoon cumin seeds

1 large white or brown onion, thinly sliced

1 tablespoon crushed garlic

2 teaspoons ground coriander

2 teaspoons garam masala

1½ teaspoons ground turmeric

3 cups cooked chickpeas (see page 13)
   or 2 × 420 g cans chickpeas, rinsed and drained

2 large potatoes, cut into cubes

2 × 400 g cans diced tomatoes

salt and freshly ground black pepper

coriander sprigs, to garnish

chapattis or naan and steamed rice, to serve

1 Heat the oil in the pressure cooker over high heat. Cook the cumin seeds for about 30 seconds until they crackle. Add the onion and cook, stirring, for 5 minutes until golden and soft. Reduce the heat to low and stir in the garlic and other spices.

2 Add the chickpeas, potatoes, tomatoes and ½ cup water. Season to taste, then close the lid and lock it. Bring the cooker to high pressure over high heat. Once high pressure has been reached, reduce the heat to stabilise pressure and cook for 15 minutes. Release the pressure using the natural-release method, unlock and remove the lid.

3 Spoon into individual bowls and garnish with a sprig of coriander. Serve with chapattis or naan and steamed rice.

Borlotti beans in tomato sauce

Look for fresh borlotti beans at your greengrocer, or use the dried ones that are readily available at the supermarket (dried beans will need to be soaked before use). Combined with tomatoes, herbs and lemon in the Greek way, these beans make a very special dish.

Serves 6 / Prep 15 mins / Cook 30 mins

400 g dried or fresh borlotti beans

⅓ cup olive oil

1 large white or brown onion, chopped

3 cloves garlic, finely chopped

2 large ripe tomatoes, diced

1–2 teaspoons dried oregano

1 bay leaf

juice of 1 small lemon

2 tablespoons chopped mint

salt and freshly ground black pepper

plenty of freshly chopped flat-leaf parsley, to serve

slices of crusty bread, toasted, to serve

sprigs of parsley, to garnish

1 If using dried beans, cover them with water in a bowl and soak for several hours or overnight, then drain before use.

2 Heat the oil in the pressure cooker over medium heat and fry the onion for 3–5 minutes, until translucent. Add the garlic and fry for a few minutes more, then add the tomatoes, oregano, bay leaf and beans. Add 1 cup water then close the lid and lock it. Bring the cooker to high pressure over high heat. Once high pressure has been reached, reduce the heat to stabilise pressure and cook for 20 minutes. Release the pressure using the natural-release method, unlock and remove the lid. Check that the beans are tender (the cooking time will depend on the quality of the beans).

3 Add the lemon juice and mint, season to taste then simmer, uncovered, for 3 minutes. Remove from the heat and stir through the parsley. The beans are best served at room temperature, so let them cool slightly then serve on slices of toasted crusty bread, garnished with parsley sprigs.

Split pea & lentil dhal

In this recipe, you'll find that the green lentils hold their shape reasonably well while the split peas turn to mush, which makes for a more interesting texture. You can sometimes buy fresh curry leaves in specialty delis, and they make a great addition to this southern Indian dish. Fry a few of them with the spice mixture to add to the dhal. Another lovely variation is tender and slightly caramelised fried onion slices.

This dhal can easily be turned into a great soup by diluting it with chicken or vegetable stock.

Serves 4 / Prep 10 mins / Cook 20 mins

1 cup green lentils, rinsed and drained

1 cup yellow split peas, rinsed and drained

2 bird's eye chillies, halved

2 teaspoons ground turmeric

2 tablespoons vegetable oil

2 teaspoons black mustard seeds

1 teaspoon cumin seeds

1 teaspoon ground coriander

2 medium tomatoes, diced

¼ cup cream or coconut cream

salt

freshly chopped coriander and warmed naan bread, to serve

1 Place the lentils and split peas in a bowl and cover with cold water. Soak for several hours or overnight, then drain before use.

2 Place the soaked lentils, split peas and 4½ cups water in the pressure cooker with the chilli and turmeric. Close the lid and lock it, then bring the cooker to high pressure over high heat. Once high pressure has been reached, reduce the heat to stabilise pressure and cook for 15 minutes. Release the pressure using the natural-release method, unlock and remove the lid. The lentils should be tender, the peas mushy, and the water mostly absorbed.

3 Meanwhile, heat the oil over medium heat in a small frying pan. Add the mustard seeds, cumin seeds and coriander, and cook for about 30 seconds, until the seeds begin to pop, then add this spice mix to the lentils and stir well.

4 Place the lentils on a low heat without covering. Stir in the tomato and cream or coconut cream and simmer for 3 minutes, until heated through. Season to taste with salt, then spoon into a serving bowl and top with the fresh coriander. Serve with warmed naan bread.

Dolmades

My favourite way to serve these is on a beautiful platter with cubes of feta, tomato and fresh mint leaves. Drizzle with olive oil and garnish with lemon.

Makes about 25 / Prep 20 mins / Cook 15 mins

about 30 fresh vine leaves or preserved vine leaves packed in brine, rinsed

⅓ cup olive oil

2 white or brown onions, finely chopped

¾ cup basmati rice

1 bunch fresh dill, chopped

¼ cup currants

½ teaspoon ground cinnamon

salt and freshly ground black pepper

juice of 1 large lemon

lemon slices, to serve

crumbled feta, to serve

1 If using fresh vine leaves, blanch them by plunging them into boiling water for a minute or two.

2 Heat half the oil in a frying pan and gently fry the onions for 10 minutes until pale golden. Add the rice, dill, currants and cinnamon, and season to taste with salt and pepper. Add the remaining oil and 1 cup water, then cover and simmer for about 5 minutes until the liquid is absorbed. Remove from the heat and allow to cool slightly.

3 Line the base of the pressure cooker with several of the vine leaves. To stuff the remaining leaves, take one and lay it out flat, shiny-side down. Spoon about 2 teaspoons of the rice mixture onto the leaf at the stem end. Trim and discard the stem, then fold in the sides and roll up the leaf tightly. Place in the palm of your hand and gently squeeze with your fingers to evenly distribute the stuffing (this also helps keep the dolmades intact during cooking). Continue with the remaining leaves and rice mixture until both are used up. Pack the stuffed vine leaves tightly into the pressure cooker as you roll them so they retain their shape.

4 Pour 1 cup water and the lemon juice over the dolmades and cover with a trivet or small plate. Close the lid and lock it, then bring the cooker to low pressure over high heat. Once low pressure has been reached, reduce the heat to stabilise pressure and cook for 7 minutes. Release the pressure using the natural-release method, leaving the lid on until the dolmades have completely cooled. Once cooled, lift them carefully from the cooker into a serving dish and serve with crumbled feta and slices of lemon.

✱ *You can vary the flavour by using sultanas or chopped dried apricots instead of currants, and oregano or mint in place of dill. If you have access to a grapevine, the medium-sized, tender leaves are best for making dolmades.*

Nasi lemak

The Malaysian name *nasi lemak* means 'rice cooked in coconut milk', but it also refers to the traditional meal of coconut rice and all the dishes that usually accompany it. In Malaysia it is particularly popular as a breakfast dish at coffee shops and roadside stalls, where it is often served with boiled eggs, fried *ikan bilis* (dried, salted anchovies) and peanuts and cucumber. A more substantial version includes a meat or vegetable curry.

    You can make the rice ahead of time if you like and reheat it in the microwave.

Serves 4 as a light meal / Prep 5 mins / Cook 10 mins

1½ cups long-grain rice

½ teaspoon salt

1 × 270 ml can light or full-fat coconut milk

1 tablespoon vegetable oil

1 cup raw peanuts

cucumber, thinly sliced lengthways, to garnish

fresh pineapple, cut into small wedges, to garnish

1 Wash the rice well then drain and place in the pressure cooker with the salt, coconut milk and 1½ cups water. Mix together, close the lid and lock it, then bring the cooker to low pressure over high heat. Once low pressure has been reached, reduce the heat to stabilise pressure and cook for 6 minutes. Release the pressure using the natural-release method, unlock and remove the lid.

2 Meanwhile, heat the vegetable oil in a frying pan over medium heat. Add the peanuts and fry them for 2 minutes until golden, then remove them from the pan with a slotted spoon and drain on paper towel. Serve coconut rice in bowls topped with a scattering of fried peanuts, cucumber and pineapple.

Lentil, beetroot & radicchio salad

A delicious salad that will really excite your tastebuds. Walnut oil adds a wonderful fragrance to salads; remember, though, to dilute it with olive oil when you use it, and store the bottle in the refrigerator as it turns rancid fairly quickly.

Serves 4 / Prep 15 mins / Cook 40 mins

1 bunch baby beetroot

1 cup puy lentils, rinsed and drained

1 tablespoon olive oil

2 white or brown onions, chopped

1 clove garlic, crushed

1 stick celery, sliced

1 cup Chicken Stock (see page 38)

salt and freshly ground black pepper

1 radicchio *or* 150 g baby spinach leaves

100 g goat's feta, broken into pieces

Walnut dressing

1 tablespoon red-wine vinegar

2 tablespoons walnut oil

1 tablespoon olive oil

½ tablespoon Dijon mustard

salt and freshly ground black pepper

1 Trim off the beetroot tops, leaving about 1 cm of stem and keeping any tiny, young leaves for the salad. Wash the beetroot thoroughly.

2 Place a trivet in the pressure cooker and add 1 cup water. Place the beetroot on the trivet, close the lid and lock it then bring the cooker to high pressure over high heat. Once high pressure has been reached, reduce the heat to stabilise pressure and cook for 15 minutes. Release the pressure using the natural-release method and remove the lid. Carefully lift out the beetroot with some tongs and, when they're cool enough to handle, slip the skins off with your fingers (wear some plastic, disposable gloves to prevent the beetroot staining your skin). Cut the beetroot into quarters.

3 Rinse out the pressure cooker and add the lentils and 4 cups water. Close the lid and lock it, then bring the cooker to low pressure over high heat. Once low pressure has been reached, reduce the heat to stabilise pressure and cook for 15 minutes. Release the pressure using the natural-release method, unlock and remove the lid. Drain the lentils and rinse them briefly under cold water.

4 Heat the oil in a large frying pan. Add the onion, garlic and celery and fry gently for 5 minutes until lightly browned, stirring frequently. Add the stock and salt and pepper to taste, then bring to a boil. Add the lentils then cover and reduce to a simmer. Cook until the lentils are tender and most of the liquid has been absorbed. Remove from the heat and let the mixture cool.

5 If using radicchio, wash well and remove any discoloured outer leaves. To make the dressing, whisk together the vinegar, oils and mustard in a bowl and season well. Toss the beetroot pieces and leaves, the lentil mixture, the radicchio or spinach leaves and goat's feta with the dressing and serve.

One-pot dinners

Chicken pot-roasted with olive oil & garlic

This is a simple and excellent way to cook a whole chicken, and will result in beautifully moist and succulent flesh. The only challenge is the search for a good chicken. I prefer to pay more for really good quality chicken and have it less often. Go for free-range or, if the budget can stretch to it, organic chicken – the flesh is firmer and it does have a better flavour.

Serves 4–6 / Prep 10 mins / Cook 20 mins

1 × 1.7 kg chicken

1 lemon, cut in half

salt and freshly ground black pepper

⅓ cup olive oil

500 g chat (baby) potatoes

1 head garlic, cloves peeled

bouquet garni of 1 bay leaf, 1 sprig tarragon
or parsley and 1 sprig lemon thyme, all tied
together in a bundle with kitchen string

green salad, to serve

1 Pat the chicken dry, including the cavity, with paper towel. Rub all over with the cut lemon. Season well with salt and pepper, then truss the legs together with kitchen string.

2 Heat the oil in the pressure cooker over medium–high heat and brown the chicken on all sides. Add the potatoes, garlic, bouquet garni, the juice from both lemon halves and ¼ cup water. Quickly close the lid and lock it, then bring the cooker to low pressure over high heat. Once low pressure has been reached, reduce the heat to stabilise pressure and cook for 20 minutes.

3 Release the pressure using the natural-release method, unlock and remove the lid. Lift out the chicken and potatoes and set aside.

4 Skim the excess fat from the pan juices. Push the softened garlic cloves through a sieve and add the pulp to the juices in the cooker to make a light sauce. Carve the chicken and serve with the potatoes, sauce and a green salad.

∗ *You can make a more substantial gravy by adding a little cream or chicken stock to the sauce, reheating it gently then garnishing it with some snipped tarragon.*

Spiced pork stew with chickpeas

Adding dried chickpeas or beans to a stew or casserole is a great way to reduce the amount of meat we eat – and they are not only delicious, but very good for you as well. If you're short of time, you can use canned chickpeas or beans for this dish instead of cooking them yourself.

   The mint, parsley and tiny cherry tomatoes added at the end give a freshness that is most welcome.

Serves 4–6 / Prep 15 mins / Cook 1 hour

1½ cups dried chickpeas

1 tablespoon olive oil

500 g diced pork shoulder

1 large white or brown onion, sliced

1 teaspoon chilli powder

1 teaspoon ground turmeric

2 cloves garlic, crushed

2 carrots, diced

salt and freshly ground black pepper

1 × 200 g punnet cherry tomatoes

1 bunch flat-leaf parsley, leaves picked
   and freshly chopped

1 small bunch mint, leaves picked
   and freshly chopped

lemon juice, to taste

1 Place the chickpeas in the pressure cooker with 3 cups water. Close the lid and lock it, then bring the cooker to high pressure over high heat. Once high pressure has been reached, reduce the heat to stabilise pressure and cook for 25 minutes. Release the pressure using the natural-release method and remove the lid. Transfer the chickpeas and cooking water to a large bowl and leave to soak while continuing with the dish.

2 Rinse out the cooker and place it over medium heat on the stove. Add the oil, then add the pork in batches and brown for a few minutes on all sides. Remove and set aside, then add the onion to the pan and sauté on low heat for a minute or so, until softened. Stir in the chilli powder and turmeric and add the garlic, carrots, and salt and pepper to taste. Return the browned pork to the cooker, then drain the chickpeas and add these along with ½ cup water.

3 Close the lid and lock it, then bring the cooker to low pressure over high heat. Once low pressure has been reached, reduce the heat to stabilise pressure and cook for 20 minutes. Release the pressure using the natural-release method and remove the lid. Fold through the cherry tomatoes, parsley and mint and continue to cook on the stove, uncovered, for another 5 minutes. Sprinkle with lemon juice just before serving.

Spanish chicken & rice

This is a Spanish-style chicken dish that uses that prize of all spices – saffron, with its gorgeous golden colour and delicate flavour. If you like, you can halve the marylands or half breasts, and don't forget the coriander at the end!

Serves 4 / Prep 10 mins / Cook 15 mins

2 tablespoons olive oil

4 chicken pieces, such as marylands or half breasts, excess fat removed

1 white or brown onion, diced

2 cloves garlic, chopped

1 cup long-grain rice, such as basmati

1 red capsicum, white insides and seeds removed, flesh cut into thin strips

1¾ cups hot Chicken Stock (see page 38)

good pinch saffron threads

salt and freshly ground black pepper

1 cup frozen peas

1 tablespoon freshly chopped coriander

1 Heat the oil in the pressure cooker and, working in batches, brown the chicken pieces on all sides over medium heat. Remove and set aside. Add the onion and garlic and cook until soft and aromatic. Add the rice and capsicum strips and cook, stirring, for 1 minute until the rice is coated with the oil.

2 Return the chicken pieces to the pan, nestling them into the rice. Add the hot stock and saffron and salt and pepper to taste. Close the lid and lock it, then bring the cooker to low pressure over high heat. Once low pressure has been reached, reduce the heat to stabilise pressure and cook for 6 minutes.

3 Release the pressure using the natural-release method and remove the lid, checking that the rice is tender. Meanwhile, drop the frozen peas into a small pan of boiling salted water and cook for 3 minutes. Drain and, just before serving, add to the rice, folding through with the chopped coriander.

Rich beef casserole

This one-pot meal is slightly more complex than some, with the pressure being stopped and started again twice, so that foods which don't require such a long cooking time can be added. This illustrates how you can adapt many of your favourite recipes to the pressure cooker. For this flavoursome casserole, chuck or shin beef are good choices.

Serves 4–6 / Prep 20 mins / Cook 1 hour

¼ cup olive oil

8 small white or brown onions or 4 large onions, cut into quarters

1 kg braising beef, cut into 3 cm cubes

1 tablespoon plain flour

1 cup red wine

2 cloves garlic, finely chopped

3–4 sprigs thyme

1 bay leaf

salt and freshly ground black pepper

500 g chat (baby) potatoes

1 bunch baby carrots or 3 medium carrots, trimmed and cut into quarters

1 punnet cherry tomatoes

freshly chopped flat-leaf parsley, to garnish

1 Heat half the oil in the pressure cooker over medium heat, and lightly brown the onions until golden, then remove and set aside. Add the remaining oil and brown the beef cubes in batches over medium–high heat. Return all the beef to the pan and sprinkle with flour. Cook, stirring, for about 3 minutes.

2 Add the wine, garlic and the herbs, and season well with salt and pepper. Close the lid and lock it, then bring the cooker to low pressure over high heat. Once low pressure has been reached, reduce the heat to stabilise pressure and cook for 20 minutes.

3 Remove the cooker from the heat and release the pressure using the quick-release or cold-water release method. Uncover, add the potatoes and quickly replace the lid, bringing the cooker back to low pressure over high heat. Once low pressure has been reached, reduce the heat to stabilise pressure and cook for another 10 minutes.

4 Remove the cooker from the heat again and release the pressure using the quick-release or cold-water release method. Uncover and add the browned onions, carrots and tomatoes. Quickly replace the lid, bringing the cooker back to low pressure over high heat. Once low pressure has been reached, reduce the heat to stabilise pressure and cook for another 5 minutes.

5 Release the pressure using the natural-release method, remove the lid, and check that everything is cooked and tender. Spoon the casserole into wide shallow bowls, scatter with parsley, and follow with a green salad.

Chicken, leek & apple pudding

You'll be amazed at how good this looks when it's turned out; the golden, flaky crust encloses a melt-in-the-mouth chicken and leek filling. To make the suet pastry for this fabulous savoury pudding, use a prepared suet mix, available from most supermarkets. The best pudding bowl to use is a non-stick metal one with a tight-fitting lid.

Serves 4 / Prep 20 mins / Cook 1 hour 10 mins

2 tablespoons plain flour

4 sprigs thyme, leaves picked and finely chopped

½ bunch flat-leaf parsley, leaves picked and finely chopped

salt and freshly ground black pepper

500 g chicken thigh fillets, trimmed of excess fat and cut into quarters

1 leek, well washed and finely sliced

1 granny smith apple, peeled and chopped

Pastry

¼ cup self-raising flour

¼ teaspoon salt

1 × 250 g packet prepared suet mix

1 To make the pastry, sift the flour and salt into a medium-sized bowl. Stir in the suet mix, add ½ cup cold water and mix to a soft dough. Turn out onto a lightly floured board and knead gently into a smooth ball. Wrap in plastic film and chill for 10–15 minutes.

2 Butter a 6-cup-capacity pudding bowl and set it aside. Roll the chilled pastry out into a circle about 35 cm in diameter, then cut one-quarter out of the circle and reserve. Take the remaining three-quarters of the pastry circle and use it to line the pudding bowl, joining up the edges by pressing them together firmly.

3 Mix together the flour, thyme, parsley, salt and pepper in a bowl. Toss the chicken pieces through this mixture until well coated. Place about a third of the seasoned chicken pieces in the pudding bowl, followed by a handful of leek and apple. Repeat twice more, adding even layers until all the ingredients are used up. Roll the reserved pastry quarter into a circle to fit the top of the pudding bowl. Lay it over and dampen the edges with water. Press the edges together to seal, then cover with a lid or some foil tied tightly with kitchen string.

4 Place the pudding on a trivet in the pressure cooker. Add 2 cups water to the pan, close the lid and lock it, then bring the cooker to high pressure over high heat. Once high pressure has been reached, reduce the heat to stabilise pressure and cook for 1 hour and 10 minutes.

5 Release the pressure using the natural-release method and unlock and remove the lid. Carefully lift out the pudding bowl, remove the lid or foil, and loosen the sides with a small metal spatula. Turn the pudding out into a serving dish with shallow sides. Serve cut into large wedges.

Chicken, potatoes & capsicum

A simple, all-in-one dish that's perfect for the cook who wants to be chatting with everyone rather than alone in the kitchen. For a really intense flavour, grill or roast the capsicums first and place them in a brown paper bag to cool, before removing the charred skins.

Serves 4 / Prep 15 mins / Cook 20 mins

1 whole chicken, cut into 6–8 pieces, trimmed of excess fat

2 tablespoons olive oil

2 red or yellow capsicums, white insides and seeds removed, flesh cut into strips

3 potatoes, cut into quarters

2 cloves garlic, finely chopped

¼ cup verjuice

salt and freshly ground black pepper

1 punnet cherry tomatoes, halved

¼ cup baby basil leaves or a few basil leaves, roughly torn

crusty bread, to serve

1 Pat the chicken pieces dry with paper towel. Heat the oil over medium–high heat and, working in batches, brown the chicken pieces on all sides.

2 Return all the chicken pieces to the cooker and add the capsicum, potato and garlic. Drizzle over the verjuice and season well with salt and pepper. Close the lid and lock it, then bring the cooker to low pressure over high heat. Once low pressure has been reached, reduce the heat to stabilise pressure and cook for 8 minutes.

3 Release the pressure using the natural-release method and unlock and remove the lid. Scatter over the halved tomatoes and cook, uncovered, for another 3–5 minutes, until the tomatoes are heated through and are starting to soften. Toss over the basil leaves, season with salt and a grinding of black pepper and serve with plenty of crusty bread.

Corned beef with vegetables

Cooked with care, a corned beef dinner is one of the most comforting meals ever, especially if served with all its traditional accompaniments like mustard and cornichons. You may even like to serve it with a creamy white sauce flavoured with capers and parsley or a good dollop of mustard, to make the meal special.

I usually cook the potatoes in the cooking liquid after the meat is cooked, but you may prefer to cook them separately and make a creamy mash to go with the corned beef.

Serves 4 / Prep 15 mins / Cook 1 hour

1.5 kg corned beef (such as silverside, rump or brisket)

1 large white or brown onion, peeled and studded with 5 cloves

2 tablespoons malt vinegar

2 tablespoons brown sugar

1 bay leaf

1 bunch baby carrots or 3 carrots, quartered

800 g chat (baby) potatoes or quartered peeled potatoes

500 g cabbage, cut into wedges

50 g butter

¼ cup chopped flat-leaf parsley

Dijon or hot English mustard, to serve

pickled cornichons, to serve

1 Place the corned beef on a trivet in the pressure cooker and add the onion, vinegar, brown sugar, bay leaf, and 2 cups water.

2 Close the lid and lock it, then bring the cooker to low pressure over high heat. Once low pressure has been reached, reduce the heat to stabilise pressure and cook for 55 minutes. Release the pressure using the quick-release or cold-water release method and remove the lid. Test the meat by inserting a skewer into the middle – it should be tender, not tough. Transfer the meat to a chopping board and leave to rest in a warm place while you cook the vegetables.

3 Add the carrots, potatoes and cabbage to the liquid in the pressure cooker. Close the lid and lock it, then bring the cooker to low pressure over high heat. Once low pressure has been reached, reduce the heat to stabilise pressure and cook for 5 minutes.

4 Release the pressure using the quick-release or cold-water release method and remove the lid. Lift the vegetables from the liquid using a slotted spoon, drain and transfer to a bowl. Toss through the butter and parsley. Cut the corned beef into thick slices and serve with the vegetables, mustard and pickled cornichons.

* *If you're serving the corned beef cold, leave it to cool completely in the cooking liquid before draining it, wrapping it in foil and chilling in the fridge. Slice thinly and serve with mustard, horseradish cream, pickles or cucumber salad.*

Chicken tagine with preserved lemon

A tagine is the Moroccan equivalent of a stew, usually fragrant with spices and often piquant with olives or preserved lemon. The name also refers to the earthenware dish with a conical-shaped lid that the dish is usually cooked in – the pressure cooker takes its place admirably in this recipe.

Serves 4 / Prep 15 mins / Cook 15 mins

4 chicken marylands, excess fat removed, each cut in two between the thigh and the drumstick

2 tablespoons olive oil

2 white or brown onions, cut into quarters

juice of ½ lemon

2 cloves garlic, crushed

¼ teaspoon saffron threads

½ teaspoon ground turmeric

3 pieces preserved lemon rind, rinsed – 2 diced, 1 cut into thin strips

1 bunch coriander, freshly chopped

½ cup freshly chopped flat-leaf parsley

salt and freshly ground black pepper

4 small potatoes, cut into quarters

crusty bread, to serve

1 Pat the chicken pieces dry with paper towel. Heat the oil in the pressure cooker over medium–high heat and, working in batches, brown the chicken pieces on all sides. Remove and set aside.

2 Add the onion, lemon juice, garlic, saffron, turmeric, diced preserved lemon and ½ cup water to the cooker. Bring to a boil and add the coriander, parsley and some salt and pepper. Stir, then add the browned chicken pieces and potatoes to the pan, spooning the sauce over as you lay them in.

3 Close the lid and lock it, then bring the cooker to low pressure over high heat. Once low pressure has been reached, reduce the heat to stabilise pressure and cook for 8 minutes. Release the pressure using the natural-release method and unlock and remove the lid. Garnish with the preserved lemon strips and serve with plenty of crusty bread.

Chinese steamed chicken

Don't be alarmed that this cooked chicken meat has a slightly pearly pink colour and the bones are a little red in the centre. This is how it should be and it's the way the Chinese love it.

Serves 4–5 / Prep 15 mins / Cook 20 mins

4 cm knob ginger, cut into thin strips

4 green onions – 2 chopped, 2 cut lengthways
    into thin strips

1 bunch coriander, leaves and stems chopped,
    plus extra to serve

1 whole chicken (about 1.7 kg)

salt

2 teaspoons sesame oil

Green onion dipping sauce

⅓ cup peanut or rice bran oil

1 teaspoon salt

6 green onions, finely chopped

2 tablespoons finely chopped ginger

1 Place a trivet in the pressure cooker and add 1½ cups water. Place a third of each of the ginger, the chopped green onion and coriander on the trivet, and another third in the cavity of the chicken. Place the chicken on the trivet and sprinkle with the remaining ginger, green onion and coriander, and season with a little salt.

2 Close the lid and lock it, then bring the cooker to low pressure over high heat. Once low pressure has been reached, reduce the heat to stabilise pressure and cook for 20 minutes. Release the pressure using the natural-release method, unlock and remove the lid.

3 Carefully lift out the chicken and transfer to a plate. Rub the chicken all over with the sesame oil, then cover loosely with foil and refrigerate until ready to serve.

4 To make the dipping sauce, heat the oil in a small saucepan on high. When the oil is hot (but not smoking), remove the pan from the heat and carefully stir through the salt, green onion and ginger. Transfer to a small bowl and let the sauce cool before serving.

5 To serve, cut the chicken into pieces using a cleaver or large, heavy knife (see instructions below) and arrange on a large serving platter. Toss together the green onion strips and extra coriander leaves, scatter over the chicken and serve with the dipping sauce.

* *To chop the cooked chicken, place the whole bird on a large chopping board and, using a cleaver or a large heavy knife, cut in half lengthways. Remove and reserve the wing joints, then remove the marylands, chopping each thigh section into three and each drumstick in two. Chop away and discard excess bone from the two breast pieces then cut each across into 2 cm slices.*

Braises & casseroles

Braised lamb shanks

Go to a French-inspired restaurant and you will often find braised lamb shanks on the menu. Clever chefs know their customers love them, as they take such a long time to cook at home. The good news is that a pressure cooker can help you turn out this delectable dish in a very short time.

Buying your lamb shanks French-trimmed (where the meat and fat is removed from the end of the shank, leaving a clean bone) dramatically reduces the fattiness of the dish.

Serves 4–6 / Prep 15 mins / Cook 40 mins

2 tomatoes

6 lamb shanks, French-trimmed
(ask your butcher to do this for you)

¼ cup plain flour, seasoned with
a generous pinch of salt and pepper

2 tablespoons olive oil

1 white or brown onion, chopped

3 carrots, thickly sliced

1 clove garlic, peeled

1 tablespoon chopped fresh oregano

grated rind of 1 lemon

¾ cup red wine

¼ cup Beef Stock (see page 38)
or Vegetable Stock (see page 39)

salt and freshly ground black pepper

1 tablespoon plain flour mixed with
2 tablespoons water (optional)

mashed potatoes and steamed green beans,
to serve

1 If you want to peel the tomatoes, drop them into boiling water for 10 seconds, then transfer them to cold water to cool. Use a small sharp knife to cut the skin around the calyx, then peel the skin away. Cut the flesh into quarters and set aside.

2 Wipe the shanks with a clean, damp cloth, then toss them through the seasoned flour, shaking off any excess. Heat half the oil in the pressure cooker over medium heat and brown the shanks two at a time. Remove and set aside. Add the remaining oil with the onion, carrot and garlic to the cooker and fry for 5 minutes, stirring occasionally. Add the tomatoes, oregano, lemon rind, wine and stock and bring to a boil, stirring well, for a few minutes. Return the lamb shanks to the cooker and season well.

3 Close the lid and lock it, then bring the cooker to low pressure over high heat. Once low pressure has been reached, reduce the heat to stabilise pressure and cook for 25 minutes. Release the pressure using the natural-release method and remove the lid. Carefully remove the lamb shanks from the cooker – the meat should be very tender and almost falling off the bone. If you would like the gravy a little thicker, heat on low, uncovered, and stir in the paste of flour and water a little at a time until thickened.

4 On each plate, place a shank on a bed of mashed potato, spoon over plenty of gravy and serve with steamed green beans alongside.

Beef in Guinness

This dish is rich in meaty flavour and wonderfully comforting. I often use it as a filling for a pie (see instructions below).

Serves 6 / Prep 15 mins / Cook 45 mins

1 kg chuck steak, trimmed of fat,
    meat cut into 4 cm cubes

¼ cup plain flour, plus 2 tablespoons extra

2 tablespoons oil

1 white or brown onion, chopped

2 sticks celery, sliced

1 carrot, cut into chunks

200 g button mushrooms, quartered

4 rashers bacon, rind removed, chopped

1 × 440 ml can Guinness

½ cup Beef Stock (see page 38)

1 tablespoon tomato paste

salt and freshly ground black pepper

1 Dust the beef pieces in flour, shaking off any excess. Heat half the oil in the pressure cooker over high heat. Brown the beef in batches then remove and set aside. Heat the remaining oil in the cooker over low heat. Cook the onion, celery and carrot, stirring occasionally, for 5 minutes until soft and lightly coloured.

2 Increase the heat to high. Add the mushrooms and bacon and cook for another 5 minutes, until the bacon is browned. Stir through the extra flour and cook for 2 minutes. Add the Guinness and stock and simmer, stirring, for 3 minutes, until the liquid has thickened slightly. Return the beef to the pan and add the tomato paste.

3 Close the lid and lock it, then bring the cooker to low pressure over high heat. Once low pressure has been reached, reduce the heat to stabilise pressure and cook for 25 minutes. Release the pressure using the natural-release method and remove the lid. Season to taste and serve.

✱ *You can go one step further and use this filling to make delicious pies (pictured right). Preheat your oven to 200°C and butter four small ramekins, about 11 cm in diameter. Thaw 2 sheets of frozen puff pastry and cut out rounds the same diameter as the ramekins. Fill the ramekins with the beef mixture, and top with the pastry rounds. Make a cross in the tops of the pastry with a sharp knife, brush with a little beaten egg and cook for 15 minutes until the pastry is puffed and golden.*

Pork curry

Tamarind is a sour fruit used widely in Indian and South-East Asian cooking. It is readily available as tamarind concentrate, a thick paste needing water added to make it into a purée for cooking. The sharp flavour nicely counteracts the rich pork in this recipe, but the same amount of lime or lemon juice could be used as a substitute.

Serves 4–6 / Prep 15 mins / Cook 30 mins

¼ cup oil or butter

1 large white or brown onion, sliced

3 cloves garlic, chopped

1–2 green chillies, chopped

3 whole cloves

1 stick cinnamon

1 tablespoon ground coriander

1 teaspoon ground turmeric

½ teaspoon chilli powder

½ teaspoon cumin seeds

2 teaspoons chopped fresh ginger

1 kg boned shoulder pork, cut into 2.5 cm cubes

2 tablespoons tamarind concentrate

1 teaspoon salt

½ cup fresh coriander leaves, to garnish

steamed rice, to serve

plain yoghurt mixed with some chopped cucumber, to serve

1 Heat the oil or butter in the pressure cooker, then add the onion and garlic and fry over medium heat until softened. Add the chilli and dry spices and fry for a further 2 minutes, stirring constantly. Toss in the ginger and pork and fry for a further 5 minutes, stirring until the meat is completely coated.

2 Mix the tamarind concentrate with ¾ cup water, and stir into the pork mixture. Season with salt, then close the lid, lock it, and bring the cooker to low pressure over high heat. Once low pressure has been reached, reduce the heat to stabilise pressure and cook for 20 minutes. Release the pressure using the natural-release method and remove the lid. Leave to stand for 5–10 minutes before garnishing with coriander leaves and serving with steamed rice and yoghurt mixed with cucumber.

Osso bucco with polenta

This is osso bucco just as it should be – tender meat, falling off the bone, in all its juicy succulence. Instant polenta, available at most supermarkets, cooks up nicely in about 15 minutes. Follow the packet instructions and, when it is soft and creamy, beat in a little butter and grated parmesan.

Serves 4 / Prep 15 mins / Cook 25 mins

4–6 slices veal shank, about 3 cm thick,
    with bone in

plain flour, for dusting

salt and freshly ground black pepper

2 tablespoons olive oil

2 cloves garlic, chopped

1 white or brown onion, chopped

1 carrot, chopped

1 large stick celery, finely chopped

1½ cups dry white wine

1 bay leaf

1 sprig rosemary

5 cm strip lemon rind

1 × 400 g can diced tomatoes

250 g instant polenta

large knob butter

½ cup freshly grated parmesan

1 Dust the veal pieces in the flour, shake off any excess and season well with salt and pepper. Heat 1 tablespoon of the oil in the pressure cooker over medium–high heat and, working in batches, lightly brown the meat on both sides and set aside.

2 Add the remaining oil to the cooker and fry the garlic, onion, carrot and celery for about 5 minutes until softened. Return the meat to the cooker and add the wine, bay leaf, rosemary, lemon rind and tomatoes. Close the lid and lock it, then bring the cooker to low pressure over high heat. Once low pressure has been reached, reduce the heat to stabilise pressure and cook for 20–25 minutes. Release the pressure using the natural-release method and remove the lid.

3 Meanwhile, cook the polenta according to the instructions on the packet, and stir through the butter and parmesan to finish. Serve piping hot, spooned into bowls with a generous amount of osso bucco on top.

✱ *For a wonderfully zesty accompaniment to this dish, make some gremolata to sprinkle over the top: mix together ½ cup finely chopped flat-leaf parsley, 1 finely chopped clove of garlic and 2 teaspoons finely grated lemon rind and serve in a small bowl on the table so people can help themselves.*

Lamb with wine & anchovy sauce

Anchovies team well with vinegar to make a robust sauce to go with lamb that never fails to please. The anchovy flavour itself is subtle, so even those who would usually steer clear of them will love this delicious dish.

Serves 6 / Prep 15 mins / Cook 50 mins

1 tablespoon olive oil

30 g butter

1 × 1.2 kg boned lamb leg, trimmed of fat

salt and freshly ground black pepper

1 clove garlic, crushed

large handful rosemary sprigs

6 anchovy fillets, finely chopped

1 tablespoon plain flour

1 cup dry white wine

¼ cup white-wine vinegar

½ cup Beef Stock (see page 38)

steamed potatoes, to serve

steamed green beans, to serve

1 Heat the oil and the butter in the pressure cooker over medium heat, and brown the lamb on all sides. Once browned, remove the lamb from the cooker, set aside in a warm place and season well with salt and pepper.

2 Add the garlic, rosemary and anchovies to the cooker and fry, stirring, for a few minutes until aromatic. Sprinkle in the flour, stirring, and let it brown lightly. Pour in the wine and vinegar, and bring to the boil, cooking until the liquid has thickened slightly. Add the stock and return the browned lamb leg to the pan.

3 Close the lid and lock it, then bring the cooker to high pressure over high heat. Once high pressure has been reached, reduce the heat to stabilise pressure and cook for 20 minutes. Release the pressure using the quick-release or cold-water release method and remove the lid.

4 Carefully turn the lamb leg over, then close the lid and lock it and bring the cooker to high pressure over high heat. Once high pressure has been reached, reduce the heat to stabilise pressure and cook for a further 20 minutes, then release the pressure using the natural-release method and remove the lid. Season with more salt and pepper if needed and serve immediately with steamed potatoes and green beans.

* *For a cheaper but equally tasty alternative, you could use lamb shoulder instead of leg. You'll need a 1 kg boned shoulder, trimmed of fat and cut into large cubes. Follow steps 1–3 above: the meat will be cooked and tender after just 20 minutes.*

Daube of beef provençale

If you can't get whole beef cheeks or chuck steak for this, use gravy or shin beef, or even blade steak, which has a good flavour and becomes beautifully tender in the pressure cooker. And don't forget the orange rind – it's essential!

Serves 6 / Prep 15 mins / Cook 35 mins

2 tablespoons olive oil

125 g thickly sliced pancetta, diced

6 whole beef cheeks *or* 1 kg lean chuck steak, cut into large cubes

1 large white or brown onion, finely chopped

2 carrots, thickly sliced

1½ cups red wine

2 cloves garlic, finely chopped

bouquet garni consisting of 1 sprig thyme, 1 bay leaf and 3 stalks parsley, all tied together in a bundle with kitchen string

2 tomatoes, cut into quarters

½ cup Beef Stock (see page 38)

1–2 × 5 cm strips orange rind

salt and freshly ground black pepper

30 g butter (optional)

1½ tablespoons plain flour (optional)

mashed potatoes, to serve

1 Heat the oil in the pressure cooker over medium–high heat then fry the pancetta for 2–3 minutes, until the fat is transparent. Add the beef and brown in batches over high heat. Return all the browned beef to the pan, add the onions and carrots, and cook for a further 5 minutes. Add the wine, garlic, bouquet garni, tomatoes, stock and orange rind and season well with salt and pepper.

2 Close the lid and lock it, then bring the cooker to low pressure over high heat. Once low pressure has been reached, reduce the heat to stabilise pressure and cook for 25 minutes. Release the pressure using the natural-release method and remove the lid – the meat should now be very tender. Use a slotted spoon to lift the meat into a deep serving dish.

3 Remove the bouquet garni from the gravy and skim off the excess fat. If you prefer a thicker gravy, combine the butter with the flour and whisk into the gravy. Bring to a boil, uncovered, then turn down the heat and simmer for a few minutes before serving. Pour the gravy over the meat and serve with creamy mashed potatoes.

❋ *For an even more intense flavour, you can marinate the meat beforehand. Place the beef in a large glass bowl with the garlic, olive oil, wine and bouquet garni and marinate in the fridge for at least 3 hours. Drain the beef before browning it, and add the marinade to the cooker along with the tomatoes, stock and orange rind as per the recipe.*

Chicken paprika

This is a simple recipe for a famous dish, which while not authentic by Hungarian standards, is nonetheless delicious and worth a regular slot in your recipe line-up.

Serves 6 / Prep 10 mins / Cook 15 mins

4 ripe tomatoes

45 g butter

6 chicken thigh fillets, halved

1 white or brown onion, chopped

2 teaspoons sweet paprika

1 tablespoon plain flour

½ cup Chicken Stock (see page 38)

1 clove garlic

1 bay leaf

salt and freshly ground black pepper

½ cup sour cream (optional)

steamed rice or noodles, to serve

1 If you want to peel the tomatoes, drop them into boiling water for 10 seconds, then transfer them to cold water to cool. Use a small sharp knife to cut the skin around the calyx, then peel the skin away. Roughly chop the flesh and set aside.

2 Melt half the butter in the pressure cooker over medium–high heat and lightly brown the chicken on both sides in batches, then remove and set aside. Add the remaining butter and fry the onion until soft. Add the paprika and cook for 1 minute, then stir in the flour, stock and chopped tomatoes. Return the chicken pieces to the pan and toss in the garlic and bay leaf, stirring well and seasoning with salt and pepper.

3 Close the lid and lock it, then bring the cooker to low pressure over high heat. Once low pressure has been reached, reduce the heat to stabilise pressure and cook for 5 minutes. Release the pressure using the quick-release or cold-water release method. Stir in the sour cream, if using, and serve straight away with steamed rice or noodles.

Braised oxtail with orange rind

My butcher now keeps oxtail on hand in his freezer, though you might have to order ahead of time so you can be sure of getting it. Cook the oxtail the day before, if possible, to improve the flavour and let the surface fat harden so that it can be easily removed.

Serves 6 / Prep 15 mins / Cook 30 mins

3 tablespoons olive oil

2 large oxtails, cut into even sections

3 large white or brown onions, cut into quarters

2 large carrots, cut into quarters

2 sticks celery, cut into 5 cm lengths

¼ cup plain flour

1½ cups red wine

bouquet garni consisting of 1 sprig thyme, 1 bay leaf and 3 stalks parsley, all tied together in a bundle with kitchen string

5 cm strip orange rind

salt and freshly ground black pepper

freshly chopped flat-leaf parsley, to serve

1 Heat the oil in the pressure cooker and brown the oxtail pieces in batches, then remove and set aside. Add the onions, carrot and celery to the cooker and fry over low heat. Sprinkle over the flour and stir to blend in, then pour in the wine and bring to a boil, stirring. Return the browned oxtail to the pan and add the bouquet garni and orange rind, and season with salt and pepper.

2 Close the lid and lock it, then bring the cooker to low pressure over high heat. Once low pressure has been reached, reduce the heat to stabilise pressure and cook for 25 minutes. Release the pressure using the natural-release method and remove the lid. The meat should be very tender and almost falling off the bone.

3 Transfer everything to a large bowl, let it cool at room temperature then cover and chill overnight. The next day, skim the thick layer of fat from the surface and return the mixture to the cooker, reheating gently. Once heated through, check for seasoning, discard the bouquet garni and orange rind, and serve piping hot, sprinkled with chopped parsley.

Ragu alla Bolognese

This is the famous slow-cooked sauce originally from Italy's Bologna, where it is also called *sugo alla Bolognese* or simply *ragu*. Making this in the pressure cooker takes hours off the usual cooking time. You can also use this rich sauce as a base for lasagne.

I like to add a little cream or butter right at the end for a more luxurious flavour.

Serves 8 / Prep 10 mins / Cook 40 mins

1 kg chuck steak or minced beef

1 tablespoon olive oil

2 white or brown onions, finely chopped

2 sticks celery, finely chopped

1 large carrot, finely chopped

150 g pancetta, chopped

1 clove garlic, crushed

1 cup dry white or red wine

1 × 420 g can diced tomatoes

2 tablespoons tomato paste

125 g per person good-quality dried spaghetti or other pasta

¼ cup cream or large knob butter (optional)

pinch ground nutmeg

salt and freshly ground black pepper

freshly grated or shaved parmesan, to serve

crusty bread, to serve

1 Finely chop the chuck steak, if using, discarding any gristle or excess fat. Heat the oil in a pressure cooker over medium heat. Fry the onion for 3–5 minutes, until soft but not browned. Add the celery, carrot, pancetta and garlic and continue to cook for another 5 minutes, until the vegetables are soft.

2 Increase the heat to high and add the chopped meat or mince and cook for 4 minutes until browned. Add the wine and bring to a boil, then stir in the tomatoes and tomato paste. Close the lid and lock it, then bring the cooker to low pressure over high heat. Once low pressure has been reached, reduce the heat to stabilise pressure and cook for 25 minutes.

3 Meanwhile, to cook the pasta, bring a large pan of salted water to a rolling boil, then drop the pasta in slowly so the water stays on the boil. Stir a few times to start with and then leave to boil vigorously until the pasta is al dente (firm to the bite). Once cooked, remove the pan immediately from the heat and drain. Do not rinse, as the sauce will not cling so readily to rinsed pasta.

4 When the ragu is cooked, release the pressure using the natural-release method and remove the lid. Immediately stir in the cream or butter, if using. Season with nutmeg and salt and pepper, toss through the just-cooked pasta, adding plenty of parmesan, and serve with crusty bread.

* *To mix or not to mix? A bowl of spaghetti topped with a big dollop of bolognese sauce doesn't have the same taste as pasta and sauce that has been tossed together over the heat before being served. The Italians call this to* saltate, *meaning sauté.*

Lamb with chickpeas, pumpkin, lemon & mint

Fresh lemon and chopped mint give this dish a wonderfully fresh tangy taste. Be sure to remove as much fat from the lamb as you can. You could also use forequarter or chump chops.

Serves 6 / Prep 15 mins / Cook 30 mins

2 tablespoons olive oil

2 white or brown onions, sliced

750 g boned lamb shoulder, cut into small cubes

2 teaspoons ground cumin

1 green chilli, deseeded and finely chopped

salt and freshly ground black pepper

½ pumpkin, peeled and cubed

2 teaspoons garam masala

1 cup cooked dried chickpeas (see page 13)
  or 1 × 400 g can chickpeas, drained

grated rind and juice of 1 lemon

¼ cup torn mint leaves

toasted flatbread and steamed rice, to serve

1 Heat the olive oil in the pressure cooker over moderate heat, then add the onions and fry gently for a few minutes until soft. Add the lamb cubes and fry until browned on all sides. Stir in the cumin and chilli, pour in 1 cup water and season well with salt and pepper.

2 Close the lid and lock it, then bring the cooker to high pressure over high heat. Once high pressure has been reached, reduce the heat to stabilise pressure and cook for 10 minutes. Release the pressure using the quick-release or cold water-release method and remove the lid.

3 Add the pumpkin, garam masala and chickpeas. Close the lid and lock it, then bring the cooker to high pressure over high heat. Once high pressure has been reached, reduce the heat to stabilise pressure and cook for another 10 minutes. Release the pressure using the natural-release method and remove the lid.

4 Stir in the lemon rind, juice, a generous grinding of black pepper and the torn mint leaves. Serve hot on a bed of steamed rice with some toasted flatbread.

Beef goulash

This is another excellent main course to prepare the night before, as it tastes even better reheated. Add the sour cream at the last moment, just before serving, or offer it separately for everyone to add themselves. I like to use smoked paprika in this dish as I love the heady flavour.

Serves 6 / Prep 15 mins / Cook 35 mins

2 tablespoons vegetable oil

1 kg stewing beef such as gravy, chuck or blade, cut into large cubes

3 large white or brown onions, chopped

salt

1½ tablespoons sweet or smoked paprika

1 cup Beef Stock (see page 38)

1 tablespoon tomato paste

1 tablespoon plain flour, mixed to a smooth paste with a little water (optional)

freshly ground black pepper

½ cup sour cream

noodles, rice or mashed potatoes, to serve

1 Heat half the oil in the pressure cooker and brown the meat in batches over medium heat, then remove and set aside. Add the remaining oil with the onions and fry for a few minutes, until soft and pale golden.

2 Return the browned meat to the cooker and stir in 1 teaspoon salt, the paprika, stock and tomato paste. Close the lid and lock it, then bring the cooker to low pressure over high heat. Once low pressure has been reached, reduce the heat to stabilise pressure and cook for 25 minutes. Release the pressure using the natural-release method and remove the lid.

3 If you'd prefer a thicker sauce, spoon out a little of the hot liquid from the cooker and add to the flour paste, then mix this together and add back to the pan. Return the cooker to the heat and simmer, uncovered, for 2–3 minutes until the sauce has thickened. Check for seasoning then just before serving, stir in the sour cream, or save for dolloping later. Serve with noodles, rice or mashed potatoes.

Steamed pork ribs with ground bean sauce

This recipe does away with the traditional wok-and-steamer method for this favourite restaurant dish. You'll find ground bean sauce at Asian stores, but if you have trouble getting it, you can use black bean sauce instead.

Ask your butcher to cut whole sparerib sections into 5 cm lengths. Then you can cut between the bones to separate each rib into small bite-sized pieces.

Serves 4 / Prep 10 mins / Cook 20 mins

¼ cup ground bean sauce

2 tablespoons dry sherry

1 tablespoon finely grated ginger

2 tablespoons cornflour

2 cloves garlic, finely chopped

2 teaspoons sesame oil

1 kg pork spareribs, cut into 5 cm lengths then
  cut between the bones to separate

freshly ground black pepper

2 tablespoons cornflour mixed with
  2 tablespoons water (optional)

steamed rice, to serve

green onion, cut into fine strips, to garnish

1 Combine the ground bean sauce, sherry, ginger, cornflour, garlic and sesame oil in a large bowl. Add the ribs and toss well to coat with the marinade. Season with pepper and set aside to marinate for 15 minutes.

2 Transfer the ribs and marinade to the pressure cooker and add ¼ cup water. Close the lid and lock it, then bring the cooker to high pressure over high heat. Once high pressure has been reached, reduce the heat to stabilise pressure and cook for 20 minutes. Release the pressure using the natural-release method and remove the lid.

3 If you would prefer a thicker sauce, transfer the ribs to a plate then stir the cornflour mixture into the sauce and return the cooker to the heat. Bring to a boil, uncovered, over medium heat and simmer until thickened.

4 Serve the ribs on a bed of rice with plenty of sauce spooned over. Garnish with green onion.

Beef strips in tomato cream sauce

An old dinner-party favourite that is essentially a cheaper version of Beef Stroganoff. It can be topped with additional sour cream and snipped chives or chopped flat-leaf parsley if you like. This is a dish that can be made ahead of time, leaving the sour cream to stir in just before serving.

Serves 6–8 / Prep 10 mins / Cook 30 mins

1 kg chuck or round steak

¼ cup plain flour, seasoned with a generous pinch of salt and pepper

30 g butter

2 tablespoons olive oil

1 large white or brown onion, finely chopped

2 cloves garlic, crushed

1 × 420 g can diced tomatoes

250 g button mushrooms, sliced

1 tablespoon Worcestershire sauce

1 cup sour cream

steamed rice, mashed potatoes or noodles, to serve

1 Cut the beef into thin strips. Toss through the seasoned flour and shake off any excess (reserving the surplus flour for later use). Heat half the butter and 1 tablespoon of the oil in the pressure cooker and brown the meat in batches, adding the remaining butter and oil when the pan gets a little dry. Set the browned meat aside.

2 Add the onions and garlic to the cooker and fry, stirring, over medium heat for 5 minutes until the onions have softened. Return the beef to the cooker and stir in the surplus flour, tomatoes, mushrooms, Worcestershire sauce and ½ cup water. Close the lid and lock it, then bring the cooker to low pressure over high heat. Once low pressure has been reached, reduce the heat to stabilise pressure and cook for 20 minutes. Release the pressure using the natural-release method and remove the lid.

3 When you're ready to serve, stir through the sour cream and heat on low, stirring, until the mixture is hot (but do not let it boil). Taste and check for seasoning, then serve with steamed rice, mashed potatoes or noodles.

Irish stew

Authentic Irish stew traditionally uses lamb neck chops, a more economical choice for a household watching its budget. Because they are a little difficult to get these days without ordering them in advance from the butcher, I have used chump chops here instead.

Serves 6 / Prep 10 mins / Cook 15 mins

1.5 kg potatoes

2 large onions, thickly sliced

1 kg lamb chump chops, trimmed of excess fat

3 carrots, cut into chunks

salt and freshly ground black pepper

1 small bay leaf

2 tablespoons freshly chopped flat-leaf parsley

2 tablespoons freshly chopped chives

1 Peel and thickly slice two of the potatoes and lay the slices in the base of the pressure cooker. Halve the rest, leaving any smaller potatoes whole.

2 Arrange the onion, chops, potato and carrot in layers over the sliced potatoes in the cooker. Season well, and add the bay leaf and 1 cup water.

3 Close the lid and lock it, then bring the cooker to low pressure over high heat. Once low pressure has been reached, reduce the heat to stabilise pressure and cook for 15 minutes. Release the pressure using the natural-release method and remove the lid. Check that everything is cooked and tender. Add the parsley and chives, taste for seasoning and serve.

Braised lamb shoulder with beans

A shoulder of lamb is one of my favourite cuts of meat, and often a better choice than a leg. It's particularly good in a pressure cooker because it fits in nicely and responds beautifully to the cooker's tenderising steam treatment.

Serves 4–6 / Prep 15 mins / Cook 1 hour

1 cup chickpeas, dried cannellini or haricot beans or 2 × 420 g cans dried chickpeas or white cannellini beans, drained and rinsed

1 tablespoon olive oil

1 small shoulder of lamb

4 cloves garlic, peeled

2 white or brown onions, cut into quarters

2 tomatoes, cut into quarters

1 cup dry white wine

1 tablespoon tomato paste

salt and freshly ground black pepper

steamed green beans tossed in olive oil or butter, to serve

crusty bread, to serve

1 If using dried beans, place them in the pressure cooker with 3 cups water. Close the lid and lock it, then bring the cooker to high pressure over high heat. Once high pressure has been reached, reduce the heat to stabilise pressure and cook for 25 minutes. Release the pressure using the natural-release method and remove the lid. Transfer the beans and cooking water to a large bowl and leave to soak while continuing with the dish.

2 Wipe the pressure cooker clean, then add the oil and brown the lamb on all sides. Add the garlic, onion, tomato, wine and tomato paste and season to taste with salt and pepper. Drain the beans and add to the pressure cooker.

3 Close the lid and lock it, then bring the cooker to low pressure over high heat. Once low pressure has been reached, reduce the heat to stabilise pressure and cook for 20–25 minutes. Release the pressure using the natural-release method and unlock and remove the lid.

4 Lift the lamb out onto a warmed serving dish and surround it with the beans and other vegetables. The lamb should be tender enough to be easily cut or pulled apart into chunks. Serve with steamed green beans and plenty of crusty bread.

Once you're confident using your pressure cooker . . .

. . . you'll be ready to try your own variations on these recipes. To help, here's my basic formula for a richly flavoured pressure-cooked soup or stew, which can be easily varied depending on what you have to hand. The amount of liquid required will vary, and will be dependent on your model of cooker as well as your own particular tastes – a little bit of trial and error may be necessary before you get it just right.

1–1.5 kg meat or poultry (such as stewing beef or lamb, including shanks, cubed pork shoulder, chicken pieces)

1–1.5 kg vegetables (such as potatoes, carrots, turnips, parsnips, leeks, onions, mushrooms, and some of the firmer green vegetables such as green beans: the firmer veg will need to be cut into large chunks; smaller or more delicate vegetables can be left whole)

1–2 cups grains or pulses (lentils, chickpeas, dried beans or rice)

aromatic flavourings and spices (such as garlic, peppercorns, a bay leaf, spices, fresh herbs, and lemon or orange rind – all of these add flavour on their own or in combinations)

Start by heating a little oil in the cooker and browning the meat or chicken. Add the vegetables, stir in the grains or pulses, and add the aromatic flavourings or spices with some sea salt and freshly ground black pepper to taste. Pour in water, wine, stock or verjuice – you'll obviously need more liquid if you're making a soup than you would for a thick stew, and remember to add at least the minimum amount your cooker requires.

Close the lid and lock it, then bring the cooker to high pressure on high heat. Once high pressure has been reached, reduce the heat to stabilise pressure and cook for 10–25 minutes, calculating the cooking time based on the longest-cooking ingredient, usually the dried beans (soaked beans generally need 10–15 minutes, unsoaked beans take 25–30 minutes). Release the pressure using the natural-release method, remove the lid and serve.

Desserts

Treacle sponge pudding

This is the kind of pudding that makes everyone's eyes light up with joy and anticipation when it's brought to the table. And because it's so comfortingly sweet and melt-in-the-mouth with its gentle tang of lemon, it doesn't disappoint.

Serves 6–8 / Prep 15 mins / Cook 1 hour

2 tablespoons golden syrup

juice of ½ lemon

1 tablespoon breadcrumbs

125 g unsalted butter

grated rind of 1 lemon

½ cup castor sugar

2 large eggs

1¼ cups self-raising flour

salt

¼ cup milk, plus extra if needed

custard, cream or ice cream, to serve

1 Butter a 5-cup-capacity pudding basin. Add the golden syrup, lemon juice and breadcrumbs to the basin and mix together.

2 Using an electric mixer or hand-held beaters, cream the butter with the lemon rind and gradually beat in the sugar until light and fluffy. Add the eggs, one at a time, beating well between each addition. Sift the flour with a pinch of salt into the creamed mixture and fold in lightly with the milk to form a batter which will drop from the spoon (add more milk if necessary).

3 Add the mixture to the pudding basin, cover with the lid, or top with a round of greaseproof paper and cover with foil to come over the edges, then secure the foil tightly under the lip of the bowl with kitchen string. Put a trivet in the pressure cooker and add 1½ cups water. Place the basin on a folded tea towel or piece of muslin. Pick up the ends of the cloth, lift the basin then carefully lower it onto the trivet. Fold the ends of the cloth over the basin and leave as it cooks.

4 Close the lid and lock it, then bring the cooker to low pressure over high heat. Once low pressure has been reached, reduce the heat to stabilise pressure and cook for 50–55 minutes.

5 Release the pressure using the natural-release method and remove the lid. Use tongs to pull out the ends of the cloth over the sides of the cooker to cool. After a few seconds, pick up the cloth ends and carefully use them to lift the basin from the cooker. Remove the lid or foil and paper and turn the pudding out onto a serving plate. Serve cut into wedges with custard, cream or ice cream.

Lemon cheesecake

Simplicity is the secret of a good cheesecake. Apart from the luscious cream cheese and the gentle nuttiness of the almond meal, all you need to flavour this is a refreshing hint of lemon. If you'd like to dress this one up a little, try topping it with thin slices of lemon cooked in a little sugar syrup, or a few soft dollops of whipped cream topped with toasted flaked or slivered almonds.

Serves 10 / Prep 15 mins / Cook 30 mins

160 g Granita biscuits, crushed

2 tablespoons almond meal

80 g butter, melted

250 g cream cheese, at room temperature

½ cup castor sugar

3 eggs, beaten

1 cup sour cream

finely grated rind and juice of 1 lemon

mixed berries dusted with sugar, to serve

1 Butter a 20–22 cm springform cake tin and cover the outside tightly with a large sheet of foil so no water can seep in. Combine the biscuits, almond meal and butter in a mixing bowl. Press this crumb mixture into the base of the prepared cake tin. Refrigerate while you prepare the filling.

2 Using an electric mixer or hand-held beaters, beat the cream cheese and sugar together until smooth, then mix in all the remaining ingredients until smooth and creamy. Spoon this mixture into the prepared tin and cover tightly with foil (being sure not to let the foil touch the filling).

3 Put a trivet in the pressure cooker and add 1½ cups water. Place the cake tin on a folded tea towel or piece of muslin. Pick up the ends of the cloth, lift the tin then carefully lower it onto the trivet. Fold the ends of the cloth over the tin and leave as it cooks. Close the lid and lock it, then bring the cooker to low pressure over high heat. Once low pressure has been reached, reduce the heat to stabilise pressure and cook for 30 minutes.

4 Release the pressure using the natural-release method and remove the lid. Use tongs to pull out the ends of the cloth over the sides of the cooker to cool. After a few seconds, pick up the cloth ends and carefully use them to lift the cake tin from the cooker. Remove all the foil and let the cake cool to room temperature. Refrigerate for 4 hours or overnight. Slide a small metal spatula around the sides to ease the cheesecake away from the tin. Transfer cheesecake to a serving plate, top with mixed berries dusted with sugar and serve.

Ruby-red quinces

Quinces usually need very long, slow cooking to turn a deep ruby-red and get that intense flavour that is so revered by food lovers. Some cooks leave them to bake overnight in the oven on a very low heat, but they are perfect for the pressure cooker as it takes just 1 hour to achieve this delicious result.

These are wonderful served as they are, or you could use them to fill a tart or chop then mix them into a butter-cake mixture just before baking, to make a cake from heaven.

Serves 8 / Prep 15 mins / Cook 1 hour

1 cup verjuice or dry white wine

2 cups castor sugar

1 stick cinnamon

5 quinces

cream, to serve

1 Put the verjuice or wine, sugar and cinnamon into the pressure cooker with 1 cup water. Place over a medium heat and bring to the boil, stirring once or twice until the sugar has dissolved.

2 Peel the quinces, cut them in quarters and core them (if you find the coring too difficult at this point, it can be done after they're cooked). As you work, place the quarters in the syrup in the cooker, turning them so that they are coated all over with the syrup.

3 Close the lid and lock it, then bring the cooker to low pressure over high heat. Once low pressure has been reached, reduce the heat to stabilise pressure and cook for 40 minutes. Release the pressure using the natural-release method and unlock the lid. Turn the quince quarters in the syrup so that the uncovered pieces turn a deeper red, and let them cool in the cooker.

4 Remove the quinces and cut away the cores if you haven't already done so. Arrange them in a shallow serving dish, pour over the syrup, then serve at room temperature or chill in the refrigerator and serve cold, with cream alongside.

Creamy rice pudding

When you first take the lid off this rice pudding, you might think it's too soupy. Take heart: once you've simmered it for a short time and then left it to stand for a few minutes before serving, it will magically turn into a creamy, delicious rice pudding.

You can easily vary the flavourings with a rice pudding such as this. Sometimes, I add a split vanilla bean or a little vanilla extract, or I might try a few bruised cardamom pods or a cinnamon stick.

Serves 6 / Prep 5 mins / Cook 25 mins (including standing time)

2⅔ cups milk

⅓ cup castor sugar

1 cup long-grain rice

1 tablespoon unsalted butter

½ teaspoon ground cinnamon

salt

ground cinnamon or freshly ground nutmeg, to serve

1 quantity Cherries in Syrup (see page 162), to serve

1 Place the milk, sugar, rice, butter, ground cinnamon, a good pinch of salt and 2 cups water into the cooker and stir to combine. Close the lid and lock it, then bring the cooker to high pressure over high heat. Once high pressure has been reached, reduce the heat to stabilise pressure and cook for 10 minutes.

2 Release the pressure using the natural-release method and remove the lid. Return the cooker to the stove and simmer, uncovered, over medium heat for 5 minutes or so, until thickened and creamy.

3 Transfer to a serving dish, sprinkle with ground cinnamon or nutmeg and leave to stand for 10 minutes, or longer if you want it even thicker. Serve warm with cherries cooked in syrup spooned on top.

Cherries in syrup

You can enjoy these lovely cherries in syrup all year round now that frozen cherries are readily available. The tart sweetness is divine with the Creamy Rice Pudding on page 160, or simply with vanilla ice cream or yoghurt.

Serves 4 / Prep 5 mins / Cook 3 mins

250 g pitted fresh or frozen cherries

¼ cup castor sugar

1 cup red wine or water

1 vanilla bean

1 If using fresh cherries, leave the stalks intact. Place the cherries, sugar, wine or water and the vanilla bean into the pressure cooker.

2 Close the lid and lock it, then bring the cooker to low pressure over high heat. Once low pressure has been reached, reduce the heat to stabilise pressure and cook for 3 minutes.

3 Release the pressure using the natural-release method and remove the lid. Transfer the mixture to a bowl and let it cool, then refrigerate until ready to use.

✳ *You might like to make your cherry syrup a little thicker so that it clings gently to the rice pudding, ice cream or yoghurt. After cooking the cherries and removing the lid, add 3 teaspoons cornflour mixed with 3 teaspoons water to the cherries, and return to a moderate heat, stirring, until it comes to the boil, then take off the heat.*

Rice custard pudding

This simple pudding is the perfect thing for tired young children (or adults) when a little pick-me-up and comfort in the form of creamy sweetness is needed. It's ideal, of course, if you have some leftover cooked rice on hand, but if not, it takes no time to cook in the pressure cooker.

Serves 4 / Prep 10 mins / Cook 20 mins

½–¾ cup steamed rice (see page 81)

3 eggs

3 tablespoons castor sugar

4 cups milk

½ teaspoon vanilla extract

15 g butter

grated nutmeg

1 Butter a 16 cm soufflé dish and spread the cooked rice in the base. In a medium-sized bowl, beat the eggs and sugar until well mixed. Add the milk and vanilla and whisk again until thoroughly mixed. Stir this mixture into the rice, dot with butter and sprinkle with nutmeg, and cover the dish tightly with foil.

2 Place a trivet in the pressure cooker and add 1½ cups water. Put the dish on a folded tea towel or piece of muslin. Pick up the ends of the cloth, lift the dish then carefully lower it onto the trivet. Fold the ends of the cloth over the dish and leave as it cooks. Close the lid and lock it, then bring the cooker to low pressure over high heat. Once low pressure has been reached, reduce the heat to stabilise pressure and cook for 20 minutes.

3 Release the pressure using the natural-release method and remove the lid. Use tongs to pull out the ends of the cloth over the sides of the cooker to cool. After a few seconds, pick up the cloth ends and carefully use them to lift the dish from the cooker. Lift off the foil and check – the custard should be set but still a little wobbly (not at all runny). Let the pudding cool for 5–10 minutes before spooning into small dessert bowls.

Stuffed apples

These stuffed apples look very pretty and can be an impressive finale to a dinner party.
The rum helps to lift the flavour and adds a bit of zing to the dish, although orange juice works
just as well. If you have time, try soaking the sultanas in the rum or orange juice for 30 minutes
or so beforehand for a richer flavour.

Serves 4 / Prep 10 mins / Cook 15 mins

¼ cup sultanas

¼ cup ground almonds

2 teaspoons grated orange rind

½ teaspoon ground cinnamon

1 tablespoon rum or orange juice

2 tablespoons brown sugar

4 large cooking apples

30 g butter

thickened cream or ice cream, to serve

1 In a small bowl, combine the sultanas, ground almonds, 1 teaspoon of the orange rind, cinnamon,
rum or orange juice and sugar.

2 Core the apples, preferably with an apple corer, cutting down to, but not right through, the base.
Scoop out a little extra flesh to make room for the filling. Score the skin all the way round the apple
with a sharp knife about a quarter of the way from the top – this stops the skin splitting during
cooking. Gently pack some fruit mixture into each apple.

3 Place each apple on a square of foil large enough to completely wrap it. Top each apple with
a quarter of the butter, then wrap the foil around the apple, pinching the ends together firmly at the
top. Place the apples on a trivet or steamer insert in the pressure cooker and pour in 1 cup water.

4 Close the lid and lock it, then bring the cooker to high pressure over high heat. Once high pressure
has been reached, reduce the heat to stabilise pressure and cook for 12–15 minutes, depending on the
size of the apples. Release the pressure using the quick-release or cold-water release method.
Remove the lid and, using oven mitts, carefully take the apples out of the cooker and remove the foil.
Sprinkle the remaining orange rind on top and serve warm with thickened cream or ice cream.

Crème caramel

This favourite dessert is wonderful in the pressure cooker, but may take a little bit of trial and error to get just right – for the perfect consistency, you may need to adjust the cooking time slightly for your particular cooker. Once you've got the timings right, you'll find this cooks like a dream, and is much simpler than cooking it in the oven.

  You can use this basic recipe to make plain baked custard by leaving out the caramel steps. You can also make a chocolate custard by adding about 50 g chopped chocolate to the milk and cream when it is scalded, stirring so that it melts.

Serves 6 / Prep 15 mins / Cook 35 mins (plus 1 hour cooling time)

1½ cups castor sugar

1 cup pouring cream

1½ cups milk

1 vanilla bean, split, beans scraped

3 eggs

2 egg yolks

1 Put 1 cup of the sugar and ½ cup water in a small saucepan over low heat until the sugar dissolves. Increase the heat and boil until golden brown. Pour the caramel into a 16 cm soufflé dish. Hold the dish with a cloth and quickly rotate it until the caramel coats the sides and base, then set aside and leave to cool.

2 Heat the cream and milk with the vanilla bean in another small saucepan until scalded (just before it reaches boiling point). Remove from the heat and let the mixture cool slightly. In a bowl, whisk the eggs, egg yolks and the remaining sugar together until well blended. Gradually pour in the cooled milk, stirring constantly, then strain through a sieve into a large jug or bowl.

3 Pour the custard into the caramel-lined dish and top with a plate or cover tightly with a large sheet of foil. Put a trivet in the pressure cooker and add 1½ cups water. Place the dish on a folded tea towel or piece of muslin. Pick up the ends of the cloth, lift the dish then carefully lower it onto the trivet. Fold the ends of the cloth over the dish and leave as it cooks.

4 Close the lid and lock it, then bring the cooker to low pressure over high heat. Once low pressure has been reached, reduce the heat to stabilise pressure and cook for 30 minutes. Release the pressure using the natural-release method and unlock the lid. Check the crème caramel is firm – if not, cook for a few minutes more on low pressure. Once cooked, release the pressure using the natural-release method and leave the crème caramel in the cooker to cool for 1 hour. Use tongs to pull out the ends of the cloth over the sides of the cooker to cool. After a few seconds, pick up the cloth ends and carefully use them to lift the dish from the cooker. Remove the foil and let the custard stand until completely cooled, then cover loosely with plastic film and chill in the fridge overnight.
To serve, slip a thin knife or metal spatula gently around the edges and invert onto a serving plate.

Chocolate & orange pudding

Soft and melt-in-the-mouth. If this is cooked just right, there should be a nice amount
of sauce inside the pudding.

Serves 6 / Prep 10 mins / Cook 30 mins

⅓ cup self-raising flour

¼ cup cocoa, plus extra for dusting

30 g butter

¼ cup castor sugar

grated rind and juice of 1 small orange

2 eggs, separated

1¼ cups milk

pouring cream, to serve

1 Butter a 16 cm soufflé dish and set aside.

2 Sift the flour and the cocoa into a bowl and set aside. Using an electric mixer or hand-held beaters,
cream the butter and sugar with the orange rind until pale and fluffy. Beat in the egg yolks, then stir
in the sifted dry ingredients a little at a time, alternating with the milk.

3 In a separate bowl, beat the egg whites until stiff, then fold lightly yet thoroughly into the
mixture with the orange juice. Pour the mixture into the soufflé dish. Cover with a plate or tightly
with a large sheet of foil, then secure the foil tightly with kitchen string.

4 Put a trivet in the pressure cooker and add 1½ cups water. Place the soufflé dish on a folded tea
towel or piece of muslin. Pick up the ends of the cloth, lift the dish then carefully lower it onto the
trivet. Fold the ends of the cloth over the dish and leave there while it cooks.

5 Close the lid and lock it, then bring the cooker to high pressure over high heat. Once high
pressure has been reached, reduce the heat to stabilise pressure and cook for 30 minutes.
Release the pressure using the natural-release method and remove the lid. Use tongs to pull out
the ends of the cloth over the sides of the cooker to cool. After a few seconds, pick up the cloth
ends and carefully use them to lift the dish from the cooker. Remove the cover, dust lightly with
cocoa, and serve hot with cream for pouring over.

Cherry clafoutis

This traditional French flan is given a new look in the pressure cooker. Usually the texture is not unlike a Yorkshire pudding – crisp and golden – but in the pressure cooker this dessert takes on a lightness that is delicious and very comforting.

Of all the summer fruits, cherries best lend themselves to cooking but, alas, the season is so short. Happily, frozen cherries are available in most supermarkets, or you may like to try canned cherries, reducing the sugar to 2 tablespoons.

Serves 6 / Prep 15 mins / Cook 40 mins

20 g butter, at room temperature

⅓ cup castor sugar

4 eggs

1 cup pouring cream

⅓ cup almond meal

1 tablespoon plain flour

150 g pitted fresh or frozen cherries (thawed)

icing sugar, to dust

1 Using an electric mixer or hand-held beaters, cream the butter and sugar until light and fluffy. Whisk in the eggs, cream, almond meal and flour until smooth. Pour into a 20 cm shallow pie dish and sprinkle the cherries on top. Cover the dish with foil to come over the edges.

2 Place a trivet in the pressure cooker and add 1½ cups water. Place the pie dish on a folded tea towel or piece of muslin. Pick up the ends of the cloth, lift the dish then carefully lower it onto the trivet. Fold the ends of the cloth over the dish and leave there while it cooks. Close the lid and lock it, then bring the cooker to low pressure over high heat. Once low pressure has been reached, reduce the heat to stabilise pressure and cook for 40 minutes.

3 Release the pressure using the natural-release method and remove the lid. Use tongs to pull out the ends of the cloth over the sides of the cooker to cool. After a few seconds, pick up the cloth ends and carefully use them to lift the dish from the cooker. Dust with icing sugar and serve.

✱ *You could make the clafoutis in individual ramekins if you like. You'll need 6 × ½-cup or 4 × ¾-cup heatproof dishes, and these individual serves will only need to cook for 30 minutes on low pressure.*

Lemon delicious

How can anything this simple be so good? Generations have enjoyed this old favourite, sometimes also called lemon surprise pudding. The charming surprise underneath the sponge topping is a creamy lemon sauce.

Serves 6 / Prep 15 mins / Cook 25 mins

30 g butter

grated rind and juice of 2 lemons

½ cup castor sugar

2 eggs, separated

⅓ cup self-raising flour, sifted

1¼ cups milk

pouring cream, to serve

1 Butter a 16 cm soufflé dish and set it aside.

2 Using an electric mixer or hand-held beaters, cream the butter with the lemon rind and gradually beat in the sugar until light and fluffy. Beat in the egg yolks, then stir in the sifted flour a little at a time, alternating with the milk. In a separate bowl, beat the egg whites until stiff and fold into the butter mixture with the lemon juice until combined. Pour into the prepared soufflé dish. Cover with a plate or tightly with a large sheet of foil.

3 Place a trivet in the pressure cooker and add 1½ cups water. Put the dish on a folded tea towel or piece of muslin. Pick up the ends of the cloth, lift the dish then carefully lower it onto the trivet. Fold the ends of the cloth over the dish and leave as it cooks.

4 Close the lid and lock it, then bring the cooker to high pressure over high heat. Once high pressure has been reached, reduce the heat to stabilise pressure and cook for 25 minutes. Release the pressure using the natural-release method and remove the lid. Use tongs to pull out the ends of the cloth over the sides of the cooker to cool. After a few seconds, pick up the cloth ends and carefully use them to lift the dish from the cooker. Remove the foil, and serve hot, spooned into bowls from the dish with a jug of pouring cream alongside.

* *The lemon sauce surprise will only be there if the pudding is cooked correctly: too long and the sauce will dry out; not long enough and there won't be sufficient sponge topping.*

Chocolate bread pudding

Here, the breadcrumbs absorb the delectable chocolate custard to make a smooth-as-silk pudding. For a sophisticated twist, you could spike the pudding mixture with ¼ cup brandy or whisky stirred in before cooking.

Serves 6 / Prep 15 mins / Cook 25 mins

2 cups milk

30 g unsalted butter, cut into pieces

125 g dark chocolate, chopped

2 large eggs

⅓ cup castor sugar

1 teaspoon vanilla extract

½ teaspoon ground cinnamon

¼ teaspoon salt

2 cups fresh breadcrumbs

icing sugar, for dusting

cream or ice cream, to serve

1 Butter a 16 cm soufflé dish and set it aside. In a saucepan, heat the milk, butter and chocolate over low–medium heat, whisking, until the butter and chocolate are melted and the mixture is smooth.

2 In a bowl, whisk together the eggs, sugar, vanilla, cinnamon and salt, then stir in the breadcrumbs. Slowly whisk in the hot-milk mixture and, when combined, pour into the prepared soufflé dish.

3 Cover with a plate or tightly with a large sheet of foil. Place a trivet in the pressure cooker and add 1½ cups water. Put the soufflé dish on a folded tea towel or piece of muslin. Pick up the ends of the cloth, lift the dish then carefully lower it onto the trivet. Fold the ends of the cloth over the dish and leave there while it cooks. Close the lid and lock it, then bring the cooker to low pressure over high heat. Once low pressure has been reached, reduce the heat to stabilise pressure and cook for 25 minutes.

4 Release the pressure using the natural-release method and unlock the lid. Use tongs to pull out the ends of the cloth over the sides of the cooker to cool. After a few seconds, pick up the cloth ends and carefully use them to lift the soufflé dish from the cooker. Remove the lid or foil and check that the pudding is set – a skewer inserted into the centre should come out clean. Dust with icing sugar and serve hot or at room temperature with cream or ice cream.

* *To make your own breadcrumbs, tear 6–7 slices of crustless white bread into pieces, then process in a food processor. They'll keep in an airtight container in the fridge for 2 weeks or frozen for 6 months.*

Pears in red wine

The best pears to use here are those hard little cooking pears that seem to take forever to ripen – the harder, the better.

This is a dessert you can easily vary. Instead of using red wine to make the syrup, try a sweet white wine, verjuice or cider, or even just orange juice. You could also try using a vanilla bean, some star anise or ginger in place of the cinnamon.

Serves 6 / Prep 10 mins / Cook 20 mins

1 cup sugar

1½ cups red wine

few strips orange rind

juice of 1 orange

2 small bay leaves

3 sticks cinnamon

6 pears, peeled

thick cream, to serve

1 Combine the sugar and wine in the pressure cooker and cook for 3 minutes, uncovered, over medium heat, stirring to dissolve the sugar. Add the remaining ingredients.

2 Close the lid and lock it, then bring the cooker to low pressure over high heat. Once low pressure has been reached, reduce the heat to stabilise pressure and cook for 15 minutes. Release the pressure using the natural-release method and unlock the lid. Cool the pears slightly in the cooking liquid, then serve at room temperature drizzled with sauce and topped with thick cream.

✱ *I love the syrup just as it is, but if you would like it a bit thicker, remove the pears from the cooker and reduce the liquid over a moderate heat for a few minutes until it has a syrupy consistency.*

Rhubarb & ginger pudding

This pudding combines rhubarb with two of its favourite companions: orange and ginger.
For puddings such as this, I use my non-stick metal bowl with its own tight-fitting lid
(it even has collapsible handles on the side to help with lifting in and out of the cooker),
but a 5-cup-capacity pudding basin or deep heatproof dish will suffice.

Serves 4–6 / Prep 15 mins / Cook 25 mins

2 stalks rhubarb, cut into 3 cm lengths

50 g unsalted butter, softened

½ cup castor sugar

⅔ cup self-raising flour

¼ teaspoon baking powder

2 teaspoons ground ginger

2 large eggs

grated rind and juice of 1 orange

10 pieces glacé ginger, sliced

thick cream or ice cream, to serve

1 Butter a 5-cup-capacity pudding basin and arrange the rhubarb pieces in the basin.

2 Put the butter, sugar, flour, baking powder, ground ginger, eggs, orange rind and juice
in a food processor and blend until combined. Stir in the glacé ginger, then pour this mixture
over the rhubarb. Cover with a lid or tightly with foil to come over the edges.

3 Place a trivet in the pressure cooker and add 1½ cups water. Put the dish on a folded tea towel
or piece of muslin. Pick up the ends of the cloth, lift the dish then carefully lower it onto the trivet.
Fold the ends of the cloth over the dish and leave there while it cooks. Close the lid and lock it, then
bring the cooker to high pressure over high heat. Once high pressure has been reached, reduce the
heat to stabilise pressure and cook for 25 minutes.

4 Release the pressure using the natural-release method and unlock the lid. Use tongs to pull out
the ends of the cloth over the sides of the cooker to cool. After a few seconds, pick up the cloth ends
and carefully use them to lift the dish from the cooker. Remove the lid or foil and loosen the sides
of the pudding with a sharp knife. Invert the pudding onto a serving dish, and serve hot or at room
temperature with thick cream or ice cream.

Bread & butter pudding

This much-loved old-fashioned pudding is the ultimate in comfort food. It's cheap to make using leftover bread and milk, and it becomes even better with a wee dram of whisky or bourbon added. It makes a big difference if the prepared pudding is left to stand for 15 minutes before cooking. This helps the bread soak up the delicious custard, giving it a sumptuous yet light, almost fluffy, texture.

I like to vary this recipe by replacing the sultanas with poached fruit such as rhubarb, cherries or blueberries – why don't you give it a try?

Serves 4–6 / Prep 25 mins (including soaking time) / Cook 20 mins

30 g butter, softened

4 thick slices bread, crusts removed

½ cup sultanas

3 eggs, lightly beaten

¼ cup castor sugar

2 tablespoons whisky or bourbon
or 1 teaspoon vanilla extract

½ teaspoon ground nutmeg

2 cups milk

1 teaspoon ground cinnamon or nutmeg

1 Lightly butter a 16 cm soufflé dish. Butter the bread on both sides, then cut into triangles and arrange half the bread in the prepared dish. Scatter with half the sultanas, then lay the remaining bread and sultanas on top.

2 Beat the eggs with the sugar, whisky, bourbon or vanilla and nutmeg. Heat the milk in a small saucepan on the stove or in a jug in the microwave until scalded (just before it reaches boiling point). Pour the milk into the egg mixture, stirring well. Strain through a sieve into the soufflé dish and leave to stand for about 10–15 minutes, or longer if possible. (If you find you have some egg and milk mixture left over, wait until the bread has soaked up some liquid and add the rest then.)

3 Sprinkle with cinnamon and cover tightly with foil, pressing the edges down firmly over the rim. Place a trivet in the pressure cooker and add 1½ cups water. Put the dish on a folded tea towel or piece of muslin. Pick up the ends of the cloth, lift the dish and carefully lower it into the cooker. Fold the ends of the cloth over the dish and leave there while it cooks. Close the lid and lock it, then bring the cooker to low pressure over high heat. Once low pressure has been reached, reduce the heat to stabilise pressure and cook for 16 minutes.

4 Release the pressure using the natural-release method and unlock the lid. Use tongs to pull out the ends of the cloth over the sides of the cooker to cool. After a few seconds, pick up the cloth ends and carefully use them to lift the dish from the cooker. Remove the foil and test by inserting a skewer into the centre of the pudding – it should come out clean. Serve warm or at room temperature.

Acknowledgements

My kitchen, and my life, would be unbearably empty without Robert, my husband of 37 years. For all this time, with most of our days spent apart because of our work, we've looked forward to the evenings and sharing a meal together. There's an easy atmosphere as we work together, with Robert doing the fine chopping and slicing, and me working on the right seasonings or herbs to use. He's always praised my cooking, and I've always been grateful for his help. I'm grateful, too, that he loves good food as much as I do. Robert has been a giant force behind this book: tirelessly testing and re-testing the recipes, checking and re-checking the copy. He did all the work; I just did the bossing and writing.

I'm enormously grateful to Lucy Nunes, who first sowed the seed for this book. Her telling me casually that all French housewives used a pressure cooker led me to give one a try, and how glad I am that I did. Lucy, by the way, has lived most of her life in Paris, so she knew all about those French housewives.

I also want to thank Julie Gibbs for having faith: she is one of those rare publishing greats that can find jewels in the most unexpected places. The book seemed to come together beautifully, thanks in no small way to Virginia Birch, who, I have had enough experience to say, is a dream of an editor. Gently coaxing, never bossy, yet all the way with her eyes on the prize – a book that's a joy to read and a breeze to cook from. Ingrid Ohlsson's ever-so-gentle resolve and determination ensured that things were kept on track, and my thanks also go to the rest of the team at Penguin, including Kirby Stalgis, Carmen De La Rue and Elena Cementon.

Thank you to Mandy Sinclair, for thinking of me as you cooked such beautiful dishes to photograph – I knew my recipes would be in safe hands. Thank you also to Mark O'Meara for the beautiful photography and Yael Grinham for the styling – you've both given a truth to the food, and helped make the book welcoming and appealing.

A

aluminium pressure cookers   3
anchovies
   Lamb with wine & anchovy sauce   131
apples
   apple sauce   7
   Stuffed Apples   165
Aromatic rice pilaf   83
artichokes
   Braised artichokes with breadcrumb stuffing   61

B

Barley risotto with chorizo & mushrooms   87
beans
   Borlotti beans in tomato sauce   90
   Braised lamb shoulder with beans   149
   Braised zucchini, beans & tomatoes   65
   dried   8
   White bean dip   15
beef
   Beef goulash   143
   Beef in Guinness   124
   Beef stock   38
   Beef strips in tomato cream sauce   146
   Beef Stroganoff   146
   Corned beef with vegetables   115
   Daube of beef provençale   133
   Ragu alla Bolognese   138
   Rich beef casserole   108
   Spicy beef chilli on warm burritos   22
beetroot
   Lentil, beetroot & radicchio salad   98
   Summer beetroot soup   49
'Blue Point' pressure cookers   4
Borlotti beans in tomato sauce   90
bouillon   37–39
Braised artichokes with breadcrumb stuffing   61
Braised lamb shanks   123
Braised lamb shoulder with beans   149
Braised oxtail with orange rind   137
Braised zucchini, beans & tomatoes   65
Bread & butter pudding   180
burritos
   Spicy beef chilli on warm burritos   22

C

Cabbage with pancetta, garlic & rosemary   69
capsicums
   Chicken, potatoes & capsicum   112
   Peperonata   73
   Tomato & capsicum chutney   33
carrots
   Peppery carrot salad   18
casseroles   8, 150
   Rich beef casserole   108
Cheesecake, Lemon   156
cherries
   Cherries in syrup   162
   Cherry clafoutis   170
chicken
   Chicken paprika   134
   Chicken pot-roasted with olive oil & garlic   102

Chicken stock   38
Chicken tagine with preserved lemon   116
Chicken, leek & apple pudding   111
Chicken, potatoes & capsicum   112
Chinese steamed chicken   118
Spanish chicken & rice   107
chicken livers
   Terrine or pâté maison   26–28
chickpeas
   Chickpea curry   88
   Hummus bi tahini   13
   Lamb with chickpeas, pumpkin, lemon & mint   140
   Spiced pork stew with chickpeas   104
Chinese steamed chicken   118
chocolate
   Chocolate & orange pudding   168
   Chocolate bread pudding   175
chorizo
   Barley risotto with chorizo & mushrooms   87
chutneys
   Date & tamarind chutney   32
   Tomato & capsicum chutney   33
cleaning your pressure cooker   6
'Clipso' pressure cookers   3
cooking times   2
Corned beef with vegetables   115
cranberries   7
Creamy rice pudding   160
Crème caramel   166
curries
   Chickpea curry   88
   Malaysian vegetable curry   70
   Pork curry   126
   Potato & pea curry   62

D

Date & tamarind chutney   32
Daube of beef provençale   133
desserts   8, 9
   Bread & butter pudding   180
   Cherries in syrup   162
   Cherry clafoutis   170
   Chocolate & orange pudding   168
   Chocolate bread pudding   175
   Creamy rice pudding   160
   Crème caramel   166
   Lemon cheesecake   156
   Lemon delicious   173
   Pears in red wine   176
   Rhubarb & ginger pudding   179
   Rice custard pudding   163
   Ruby-red quinces   159
   Stuffed apples   165
   Treacle sponge pudding   155
dhal
   Split pea & lentil dhal   93
dips
   Peppery carrot salad   18
   Spicy eggplant & tomato   25
   White bean dip   15
Dolmades   94

E

eggplant
   Eggplant with tomato, raisins & feta   66

Spicy eggplant & tomato   25
Eggs & spinach in ramekins   17
'Europe' pressure cookers   3
Evinox brand pressure cooker   3

F
Fagor brand pressure cooker   3
fish
Fish stock   39
Portuguese fish soup   50
Salmon bread soufflé   21
Fissler brand pressure cooker   4
French onion soup   45

G
gaskets   5
Gypsy vegetable stew   76

H
ham
Split pea & ham soup   54
Hummus bi tahini   13

I
Irish stew   147

K
Kuhn Rikon brand pressure cooker   3

L
lamb
Braised lamb shanks   123
Braised lamb shoulder with beans   149
Irish stew   147
Lamb with chickpeas, pumpkin, lemon & mint   140
Lamb with wine & anchovy sauce   131
Scotch broth   53
lemon
Lemon cheesecake   156
Lemon delicious   173
lentils
Lentil tapenade   14
Lentil, beetroot & radicchio salad   98
Spinach, lemon & lentil soup   46
Split pea & lentil dhal   93
liquids   4–5, 7, 8

M
Malaysian vegetable curry   70
Marmalade, Onion   31
meats   8
mushrooms
Barley risotto with chorizo & mushrooms   87
Risotto bianco   84

N
Nasi lemak   97

O
onions
French onion soup   45
Onion marmalade   31
Osso bucco with polenta   128
oxtail
Braised oxtail with orange rind   137

P
pasta   7
pâtés
Pâté maison   26–28
Pork pâté   29
Pears in red wine   176
peas
Potato & pea curry   62
Split pea & ham soup   54
Split pea & lentil dhal   93
Velvet pea & zucchini soup   40
Peperonata   75
Peppery carrot salad   18
'Perfect' pressure cookers   4
polenta
Osso bucco with polenta   128
pork
Pork curry   126
Pork rillettes   29
Spiced pork stew with chickpeas   104
Steamed pork ribs with ground bean sauce   144
Terrine or pâté maison   26–28
porridge   7
Portuguese fish soup   50
potatoes
Chicken, potatoes & capsicum   112
Potato & pea curry   62
Potatoes braised with tomatoes & oregano   74
Pressure-roasted potatoes   58
Rocket & potato soup   42
pressure cookers
brands   3–4
choosing   3–4
cleaning   6
discolouration   9
handles   3
lifting dishes from   7
opening lid   6
pressure levels   5–6
release methods   6, 9
size   3
storing   7
using   4–6
pressure cooking
cooking times   2
suitable foods   8
technique   2, 4–6
troubleshooting   8–9
unsuitable foods   7
puddings
Bread & butter pudding   180
Chocolate & orange pudding   168
Chocolate bread pudding   175
Creamy rice pudding   160
Rhubarb & ginger pudding   179

Rice custard pudding   163
Treacle sponge pudding   155

Q

Quinces, Ruby-red   159

R

radicchio
   Lentil, beetroot & radicchio salad   98
Ragu alla Bolognese   138
'Rapid' pressure cookers   3
rhubarb   7
   Rhubarb & ginger pudding   179
rice   8
   Aromatic rice pilaf   83
   Creamy rice pudding   160
   Dolmades   94
   Nasi lemak   97
   Rice custard pudding   163
   Risotto bianco   84
   Spanish chicken & rice   107
   steamed   81
   steamed cardamom   81
Rich beef casserole   108
risotto   8
   Barley risotto with chorizo & mushrooms   87
   Risotto bianco   84
Rocket & potato soup   42
Ruby-red quinces   159

S

safety   7
salads
   Lentil, beetroot & radicchio salad   98
   Peppery carrot salad   18
Salmon bread soufflé   21
Scotch broth   53
soufflés
   Salmon bread soufflé   21
soups   8
   basic recipe   150
   French onion soup   45
   Portuguese fish soup   50
   Rocket & potato soup   42
   Scotch broth   53
   Spinach, lemon & lentil soup   46
   Split pea & ham soup   54
   Summer beetroot soup   49
   Velvet pea & zucchini soup   40
Spanish chicken & rice   107
Spiced pork stew with chickpeas   104
Spicy beef chilli on warm burritos   22
Spicy eggplant & tomato   25
spinach
   Eggs & spinach in ramekins   17
   Spinach, lemon & lentil soup   46
split peas
   Split pea & ham soup   54

Split pea & lentil dhal   93
stainless steel pressure cookers   3
Steamed pork ribs with ground bean sauce   144
steamer basket   5
stews   8, 9
   basic recipe   150
   Gypsy vegetable stew   76
   Irish stew   147
   Spiced pork stew with chickpeas   104
stocks   8, 37–39
   Beef stock   38
   Chicken stock   38
   Fish stock   39
   Vegetable stock   39
storing your pressure cooker   7
stovetops   2
Stuffed apples   165
Summer beetroot soup   49

T

tahini
   Hummus bi tahini   13
tamarind
   Date & tamarind chutney   32
   Pork curry   126
Tapenade, Lentil   14
Tefal brand pressure cooker   3
temperature   2
Terrine   26–28
times, cooking   2
tomatoes
   Braised zucchini, beans & tomatoes   65
   Eggplant with tomato, raisins & feta   66
   Potatoes braised with tomatoes & oregano   74
   Spicy eggplant & tomato   25
   Tomato & capsicum chutney   33
Treacle sponge pudding   155
trivet   5

V

veal
   Osso bucco with polenta   128
vegetables   8, 9
   Gypsy vegetable stew   76
   Malaysian vegetable curry   70
   Vegetable stock   39
Velvet pea & zucchini soup   40
'Vitavit Royal' pressure cookers   4

W

White bean dip   15
WMF range pressure cookers   4

Z

zucchini
   Braised zucchini, beans & tomatoes   65
   Velvet pea & zucchini soup   40

VIKING

Published by the Penguin Group
Penguin Group (Australia)
250 Camberwell Road, Camberwell, Victoria 3124, Australia
(a division of Pearson Australia Group Pty Ltd)
Penguin Group (USA) Inc.
375 Hudson Street, New York, New York 10014, USA
Penguin Group (Canada)
90 Eglinton Avenue East, Suite 700, Toronto, Canada ON M4P 2Y3
(a division of Pearson Penguin Canada Inc.)
Penguin Books Ltd
80 Strand, London WC2R 0RL England
Penguin Ireland
25 St Stephen's Green, Dublin 2, Ireland
(a division of Penguin Books Ltd)
Penguin Books India Pvt Ltd
11 Community Centre, Panchsheel Park, New Delhi – 110 017, India
Penguin Group (NZ)
67 Apollo Drive, Rosedale, North Shore 0632, New Zealand
(a division of Pearson New Zealand Ltd)
Penguin Books (South Africa) (Pty) Ltd
24 Sturdee Avenue, Rosebank, Johannesburg 2196, South Africa

Penguin Books Ltd, Registered Offices: 80 Strand, London, WC2R 0RL,
England

First published by Penguin Group (Australia), 2009

ISBN 978-0-718-15633-6

Text copyright © Suzanne Gibbs 2009
Photographs copyright © Mark O'Meara 2009

The moral right of the author has been asserted

Design by Kirby Stalgis © Penguin Group (Australia)
Photography by Mark O'Meara
Styling by Yael Grinham, additional styling by Kristine Duran-Thiessen
Cover styling by Kate Brown
Typeset in 10.5/14pt Apollo by Post Pre-press Group, Queensland
Colour reproduction by Splitting Image Colour Studio Pty Ltd, Victoria
Printed in China by SNP Leefung

This edition produced for The Book People Ltd, Hall Wood Avenue,
Haydock, St Helens WA11 9UL

National Library of Australia
Cataloguing-in-Publication data:

Gibbs, Suzanne.
The pressure cooker recipe book / Suzanne Gibbs.
9780670073184 (pbk.)
Includes index.
Pressure cookery.

641.587

penguin.com.au